CRITIFICTION

SUNY Series in Postmodern Culture
Joseph Natoli, Editor

CRITIFICTION

Postmodern

Essays

Raymond Federman

State University of New York Press

Cover photo by Werner Bern.

Earlier versions of four of these essays have been published previously.
The author gratefully acknowledges the following sources: *Partisan
Review* (1973), "Surfiction: A Position"; *New Literary History* (1976), "Imag-
ination As Plagiarism"; *Humanities in Society* (1978), "Fiction Today or The
Pursuit of Non-knowledge"; *Columbia Literary History of the United States*
(1988), "Self-Reflexive Fiction."

Published by
State University of New York Press, Albany

© 1993 State University of New York

For information, address State University of New York
Press, State University Plaza, Albany, N.Y., 12246

Production by E. Moore
Marketing by Theresa A. Swierzowski

Library of Congress Cataloging-in-Publication Data

Federman, Raymond.
    Critifiction : postmodern essays /
Raymond Federman.
        p.   cm. — (SUNY series in postmodern culture)
    ISBN 0-7914-1679-8. — ISBN 0-7914-1680-1 (pbk.)
    1. Fiction—20th century—History and criticism. 2. Postmodernism
(Literature) I. Title. II. Series.
PN3503.F43 1993
809.3'045—dc20   92-44360
                                                                         CIP

10 9 8 7 6 5 4 3 2 1

For Jerry, Jurek, Larry
who will know why

CONTENTS

1. FICTION TODAY OR THE PURSUIT OF NON-KNOWLEDGE

> *Reality, whether approached imaginatively, or empirically remains a surface, hermetic. Imagination, applied to what is absent, is exercised in a vacuum and cannot tolerate the limits of the real*
> —Samuel Beckett

TO BEGIN: some thoughts, pieces of thoughts—for one never knows where one's thoughts originate, and when these thoughts merge with those of others, where one's language begins and where it converges with that of others within the dialogue all of us entertain with ourselves and with others.

1. In the beginning was not **MIMESIS** (the art of imitation), but the necessity to achieve **MIMESIS**.
2. Artistic activity begins when man finds himself face to face with the visible world as with something immensely egnimatical. In the creation of a work of art, man engages in a struggle with Nature not for his physical but for his mental existence.
3. The reality of imagination is more real than reality without imagination, and besides reality as such has never really interested anyone, it is and has always been a form of disenchantment. What makes reality fascinating is the imaginary catastrophe that hides behind it.
4. Contemporary works of fiction are often experienced with a certain anxiety, not because they threaten to extinguish the novel or the short story as recognizable genres, but because they challenge the traditional bases of both cultural and aesthetic judgment. Literature has most often been accepted as culturally significant to the extent that it

represents the external world, either through the depiction of a socio/historical situation, or through the verbalization of psychological states. Much of contemporary fiction does not relate the reader directly to the external world (*reality*), nor does it provide the reader with a sense of lived experience (*truth*), instead contemporary fiction dwells on the circumstances of its own possibilities, on the conventions of narrative, and on the openness of language to multiple meanings, contradictions, paradoxes, and irony.

In other words, at the center of the discussion (or perhaps one should say, the controversy) which has been going on now for more than four decades about NEW (innovative/experimental) FICTION versus OLD (traditional/realistic) FICTION is the problem of REPRESENTATION, that is to say the relationship of fiction to reality and life: MIMESIS.

As soon as a work of fiction refuses deliberately TO REPRESENT the world (*to mirror reality*), or refuses TO EXPRESS the innerself of man (*to mirror the soul*), it is immediately considered a failure, quickly labeled experimental, and therefore declared irrelevant, useless, boring, unreadable, and of course unmarketable.

According to the traditional view of fiction, there lies at the base of a text (a novel, a story), like an irreducible foundation, an established meaning (A SOMETHING-TO-BE-SAID) constituted even before the work is completed. This preexisting meaning affects two domains: the SELF and the WORLD.

The manifestation of this established meaning is thus divided into two parallel ideas: the aspects of the self are expressed, the aspects of the world are represented. Although still dominant today in much of literature, this concept of a text, with its two key notions of expression and representation, is highly inconsistent.

It rose to its height in a precise historical period: the nineteenth century—an era too recent for the still-innumerable believers of the EXPRESSION/REPRESENTATION DOCTRINE to see how they fit into a long and obsolete tradition, but already an era too distant for its believers to have maintained any freshness of vision.

As we learned in our schoolbooks, two literary movements dominated the nineteenth century: ROMANTICISM dealt with expression, REAL-

ISM with representation. To oppose these two movements, as it is too often done in literature courses, in term-papers, dissertations, and manuals of literary history, is to hide the fact that Romanticism and Realism are really two faces of the same coin. Both subordinate the literary text to an already established meaning present in the world even before the poem or the novel is written. It is not by chance that Victor Hugo's poems which were called *"mirrors of the soul"* find a parralel in Balzac's novels which he himself called *"mirrors that one drags along the road of reality."* [The sarcasm here is not meant to demean the greatness and the relevance of Balzac's novels or Victor Hugo's poems—these writers lived and wrote in the nineteenth century; we live and write in the twentieth century, in fact almost in the twenty-first century. Our relation to the world (however real or unreal it may be) has undergone radical changes].

This expression/representation doctrine is, of course, still with us, or at least it was the dominant and valid view of the literary act until the end of the EXISTENTIALIST ERA (sometime at the beginning of the 1950s). It is only with the advent of what has been called New Fiction, Antifiction, Metafiction, Postmodern Fiction, or what I prefer to call Surfiction, that this view began to be questioned, challenged, undermined, and even rejected.

In fact, one can consider the New Fiction that begins to take shape in the middle of the 1950s and which is still being written today in many parts of the world, as fitting into the POST-EXISTENTIALIST ERA, suggesting thereby that this New Fiction (*Nouveau Roman*, it was called in France in the 50s) turned its back on Reality, Life, and Man, or at least on the notion that fiction should only express or represent Reality, Life, and Man.

In order to understand how the New Fiction functions, and why it turned away from its own tradition, it is necessary to return for a moment to that EXISTENTIALIST ERA—that period which immediately preceded, traversed, and followed World War II—and examine its literary vision.

In 1947, Jean-Paul Sartre raised a crucial question for anyone seriously involved in literature as a creator, a critic, or simply as a student. He asked: **What is Literature?** (*Qu'est-ce que la littérature?*) Not only a question, but a lengthy essay which served first as an introduction to *Les*

Temps Modernes (the literary journal Jean-Paul Sartre launched in 1947), and which subsequently became the volume entitled *Situations* II. At the center of this essay Sartre argued the question of literary commitment—**engagement.**

The whole problematic of the *Nouveau Roman* in France during the 1950s, but also of all literary activities since World War II anywhere in the world, can only be postulated in function of Sartre's fundamental concept of literary commitment—what he called *la littérature engagée.*

What did Sartre propose?

1. An optimistic and rationalistic conception of literary activities.
2. The book as a means of communication.
3. Literature as *une prise de position*—a stance on all moral, social, and political questions.
4. The writer as participating in the shaping of history.
5. Writing as a form of liberation, a force that liberates others from moral, social, and political oppression.

This is certainly a most noble set of propositions. It means that the writer can function within this set of rules only if he participates in history in the sense of a universal event relating to individual freedom. Therefore, the act of writing is accomplished within the narrow space of a relative possibility. The writers fulfills the essential demands of his function and of his art only when he unmasks our world—that world which is but an immense mechanism of injustices.

Since the writer cannot escape his time, he must embrace it. Literature, here and now, prepares the social and socialistic revolution [*one must remember that Sartre was writing at the time from a Marxist point of view*]. Literature, he went on to argue, becomes a conquest of total freedom for everyone. It prepares the freedom of the future.

These are indeed beautiful thoughts, and yet, in spite of their impact at the time, in spite of all the debates around them, the literature (and especially fiction) that followed these pronouncements, in France particularly, but everywhere else as well, did not respect Jean-Paul Sartre's ideas.

Instead of getting involved with the **CRISIS OF CONSCIENCE** and the **CRISIS OF CONSCIOUSNESS** which underline Sartre's proposal, the literature of the last forty-five years concerned itself with itself, with literature, with the crisis of literature, with the crisis of language and of communication, with the crisis of knowledge, and not with social and political problems—except for a few rare cases in specific places and situations (in Germany, for instance, at least for a decade or so following World War II, in South Africa, or in certain Latin American countries). Everywhere else, the novel per se—that is to say the New Fiction—turned its back on Jean-Paul Sartre and the Existentialist vision.

In fact, that New Fiction [*poetry, of course, had already done so more than a century ago when it was declared useless by the Bourgeoisie*] moved from a moral and ethical purpose to an aesthetic and formalistic level to tell us, to show us, to repeat endlessly, that writers write simply to reveal the impossibility of writing in a postmodern era.

Alain Robbe-Grillet, Michel Butor, Robert Pinget, Georges Perec, Claude Simon, Nathalie Sarraute, and many others (including the great Samuel Beckett) in France; John Barth, John Hawkes, William Gass, Donald Barthelme, Robert Coover, Ronald Sukenick, Walter Abish, and many others (including myself, I suppose), in the United States; but also Italo Calvino, Julio Cortazar, Jorge Luis Borges, Severo Sarduy, Jürgen Becker, Peter Handke, B. S. Johnson, Christine Brooke-Rose, and may others all over the world (the Western World), seemed to be more concerned with the problems of writing their books, of letting the difficulties of writing fiction transpire in the fiction itself, rather than commit themselves to the problems of Man and of the injustices of society.

But this is not new. This deliberate refusal to confront social consciousness in favor of the crisis of literature goes way back to the beginning of the century: to Marcel Proust, certainly, in fiction, and to Mallarmé, in poetry. Proust who wrote a fifteen volume novel (over three thousand pages) to ask himself what it meant to write a novel; Mallarmé who, in questioning the act of writing poetry, dismantled conventional prosody and brought poetry to an impasse of self-negation from which it has not been able to extricate itself. However, Proust and his contemporaries managed to escape the failure implicit in their undertaking, whereas the new novelists seem to make of failure an occasion, or, as Samuel Beckett so well exemplified in his work, to reveal that to be a writer is to be willing to admit the inevitability of failure.

But the fact that failure is an indeniable aspect of contemporary art had already been stated, quite forcefully and movingly, in 1923, by a young, unknown French poet in a series of letters he wrote to Jacques Rivière, the editor of a French magazine (*La Nouvelle Revue Française*) who had rejected some of his poems. I mean, of course, Antonin Artaud whose poems had been refused by Jacques Rivière. The correspondence between Artaud and Rivière remains an important set of documents concerning the crisis of literature in the twentieth century.

Artaud had written in one of his poems:

> All communications are cut
> in front
> behind
> all around
> and the last ties which still cling to man must be cut
> we are without roots

And in one of the letters to Jacques Rivière he states: "I suffer from a frightening sickness of the mind. My thoughts abandon me—from the simple fact of thinking to the exterior fact of materializing thoughts into words, there is something that destroys my thoughts, something that prevents me from being what I could be, and which leaves me . . . in suspense."

Suddenly literature becomes the explanation of why the writer cannot write, why he constantly confronts the failure of expression and communication, why he can no longer represent the world faithfully and truthfully.

This is indeed the dilemma which many writers encountered throughout the first half of the twentieth century, especially those who were considered avant-garde: James Joyce, Franz Kafka, Louis-Ferdinand Céline, André Gide, Thomas Mann, John Dos Passos, William Faulkner, and Jean-Paul Sartre himself. Even though these writers wanted to affirm human dignity, they were forced to do so at times in a somewhat fragmented and seemingly incoherent style. However, these writers, and many others too, starting with Proust, managed to transfer their dilemma to their characters, and not to the writing itself, as is the case in much of the New Fiction.

It is Edouard, the fictitious novelist of André Gide's *Les Faux-monnayeurs* *(The Counterfeiters)* who confronts the crisis of writing and as such becomes a pathetic, almost tragic figure, while Gide, the real novelist, pretends playfully to have relinquished his responsibility toward the novel and its characters. It is Philip Quarles, in Aldous Huxley's *Point Counter Point*, who struggles with the creation and failure of fiction while the real author laughs at him. And there are similar writers-protagonists in novels by Thomas Mann, James Joyce, Louis-Ferdinand Céline who confront the failure of their own fictitious world. Even Roquentin, in Sartre's *La Nausée*, eventually abandons out of despair the book he is writing.

But if Antonin Artaud expressed, in a kind of lucid madness, the writer's dilemma, if his own works, which he called "these incredible rags," reveal the obstacles, denounce the limits, pinpoint the lacks, expose the inadequacies of language, they do so with such lucidity, that ultimately Artaud found in failure a reason to go on writing. In other words, like many of his contemporaries, he pursued his work with clairvoyance in the most opaque region of imagination.

Nevertheless, from Proust to Beckett, there is a feeling that something is wrong with literature, something is wrong with the act of expressing. "There is no communication," writes Beckett in 1930 in his monograph on Proust, "because there are no vehicles of communication." And even Sartre points to this crisis of communication when he writes at the beginning of his 1947 essay:

> *There has been a crisis of rhetoric, then a crisis of language. Most writers have now resigned themselves to being mere nightingales. Most writers now insist that the secret goal of all literature is the destruction of language, and to reach this goal one merely needs to speak to say nothing.*

Sartre, of course, is being sarcastic here, but this statement almost reads like a manifesto for the New Fiction. However, in spite of all the anguish, of all the anxiety of literature in the first half of the twentieth century in facing up to its crisis, it is the New Fiction (and to some extent the New Theater which received the unfortunate name of THEATER OF THE ABSURD) which made the most homogeneous effort to demystify and expose the problem, and destroy those social and cultural reflexes which kept literature blind to its own crisis.

How can the writer, then, in the light of what I have just stated, confront the human condition? How can the writer today cope with his subject? That is to say reality, Man, and social injustices. He can either follow Sartre's suggestion and become a social worker of literature, and simply write political pamphlets [or make speeches standing on top of a garbage can, as Sartre himself did in 1968, during the failed student uprising]; or else he can stop writing and become a politician [mayor of New York City, as Norman Mailer once tried], or Minister of Cultural Affairs [as André Malraux did in order to give Paris a face-lift], or flirt with the possibility of becoming a member of the government [as Günter Grass repeatedly attempted for the past forty years of so]. Or else, the writer confronts the real problem, the crisis of literature today, at the risk of losing his audience, and of locking himself into pure formalism.

Baffled by the world in which he lives, the writer is plunged into a state of anguish—intellectual anguish—because he does not comprehend that world any more, or rather because the more he knows about the world the less it makes sense. The writer knows nothing or comprehends nothing because there is nothing more to know or comprehend, or rather because there is too much to know and comprehend. In any event, absolute knowledge, like absolute truth, no longer exists. This does not mean, however, that the contemporary writer has become a nihilist, as many antagonistic critics of the New Fiction have claimed. Nihilism implies that there is nothing, and that's it. Whereas in our present state of intellectual anguish we realize that there is either too much to know, hence the confusion, or nothing more to know, hence the impossibility and futility of writing in the same old forms, but this is no cause for despair. In the impossibility of literature today, the writer also discovers the necessity of going on with literature, not simply to affirm a knowledge which is constantly slipping away, but to make of literature an act of survival.

Since the Greeks, literature has constituted itself as the vehicle of knowledge in the form of apologies, commentaries, amplifications on other texts, decorations or explanations of knowledge. In other words, literature was an affirmation of faith, of certitude in knowledge. Literature was in fact knowledge, and therefore:

> *Most works of fiction achieved coherence and meaningfulness through a logical accumulation of facts about specific situations and, more or less, credible characters. In the process of recording, or gradually revealing*

mental and physical experiences, organized in an aesthetic and ethical form, these works progressed toward a definite goal—the revelation of knowledge. To read a novel was to learn something about the world and about man.

This statement is quoted from *Journey to Chaos* [a book I published in 1965, devoted to the fiction of Samuel Beckett], in which I go on saying that "Beckett's novels seem to progress in exactly the opposite direction, retracting knowledge, canceling knowledge, dragging us slowly and painfully toward chaos and meaninglessness."

This is also the case with most works of contemporary fiction known as avant-garde or experimental. The more pages we accumulate to the left as we read a novel, let's say by Alain Robbe-Grillet [*Jealousy*, for instance] or Walter Abish [*Alphabetical Africa*], the less we seem to know. As we read we encounter repetition after repetition, the text circles upon itself, cancels itself, and instead of moving toward a resolution or a conclusion, it seems to stumble relentlessly toward a gap at the center of the book, toward a GREAT HOLE. Thomas Pynchon's *Gravity's Rainbow* also leads us toward deliberate confusion and chaos. There are many such contemporary novels that make a shamble of traditional epistemology, and do so with effrontery and even playfulness, as for instance my own novel *Take It or Leave It*.

Therefore, the question can be asked: can there be a literature that refuses to represent the world or to express the inner-self of man? The entire oeuvre of Samuel Beckett is but that. Molloy (that grandiose figure of postmodern fiction, in Beckett's novel by that title) seems to be speaking for contemporary writers when he says:

> *For to know nothing is nothing, not to want to know anything likewise, but to be beyond knowing anything, to know you are beyond knowing anything, that is when peace enters into the soul of the incurious seeker.*

Today's New Fiction seeks to avoid knowledge deliberately, particularly the kind of knowledge that is received, approved, determined by conventions. In order to succeed (paradoxically one might say) in this **pursuit of non-knowledge**, the New Fiction invents its own reality, cuts itself off from referential points with the external world. The New Fiction affirms its own autonomy by exposing its own lies: it tells stories that openly claim to be invented, to be false, inauthentic; it dismisses absolute knowledge and what passes for reality; it even states, defiantly, that reality as such does not exist, that the idea of reality is an imposture.

Ronald Sukenick, one of the leading experimental fictioneers in the United States, has one of his characters (himself a novelist) state in a collection of stories appropriately entitled *The Death of the Novel and Other Stories*:

> *Fiction constitutes a way of looking at the world. Therefore I will begin by considering how the world looks in what I think we may now begin to call the contemporary post-realistic novel. Realistic fiction presupposes chronological time as the medium of a plotted narrative, an irreducible individual psyche as the subject of its characterization, and, above all, the ultimate concrete reality of things as the object and rationale of its description. In the world of post-realism, however, all of these absolutes have become absolutely problematic.*

> *The contemporary writer—the writer who is acutely in touch with the life of which he is part—is forced to start from scratch: reality does not exist, time does not exist, personality does not exist.*

What replaces knowledge of the world and of man is the act of searching (researching even) within the fiction itself for the implications of what it means to write fiction. This becomes an act of self-reflection, and therefore fiction becomes the metaphor of its own narrative progress. It establishes itself as it writes itself. In other words, fiction now becomes a continual probing of its own medium, but a probing that cancels, erases, abolishes whatever it discovers, whatever it formulates as it is performed.

In his novel entitled *Out*, Ronald Sukenick [not the real author, but the mythical author-protagonist by that name] states: "I want to write a novel that changes like a cloud as it goes along." In my own novel *Take It or Leave It*, the narrator whose name is Federman replies to Sukenick: "I want to write a novel that cancels itself as it goes along."

These two statements suggest a kind of writing which negates whatever transitory conclusions it makes, and in fact both novels illustrate their own system of self-cancellation, and playfully acknowledge their denial of absolute knowledge—*Out* by a process of diminution and disappearance, that of the count-down; *Take It or Leave It* by a process of digression and erasure, described in the novel as **the leapfrog technique.**

To some extent these novels function like scientific research whereby one experiment after another abolishes the truths of yesterday. And it is true that more and more we have come to recognize that modern art cancels itself as it is created. The Tinguely machine is set in motion in order to destroy itself in front of the viewers. The white canvas of Abstract Expressionism pretends to deny its own existence. Avant-garde music abolishes itself into discordance or silence. Concrete poetry empties itself of meaning, while New Fiction writes itself into nonsense and non-knowledge, or to play on the title of a Beckett text: fiction seeks LESSNESSness.

Modern Art and New Fiction reveal that we exist in a temporary situation, surrounded by temporary landscapes. Faced with this transitory aspect of life and of the world, literature confronts its own impossibility. But since writers go on writing (fiction or poetry) in spite of this impossibility, it can also be said that literature, nonetheless, continues to search for new possibilities. It searches, within itself, for its subject, because the subject is no longer outside the work of art, it is no longer simply Nature or Man.

As a result we now have poems of poetry, theater of theater, novels of novel. For instance, the poem/explication of John Ashbery and Francis Ponge; the play-within-the-play of Jean Genet; the novel in spiral [*en abîme*] that circles around its own interrogations of John Barth, Walter Abish, Michel Butor, Julio Cortazar. But going even further, novels are written without characters (George Chambers, Maurice Roche, Georges Perec), and even without pronominal persons (Philippe Sollers, Samuel Beckett, Raymond Federman). There now exists a literature that appropriates objects rather than inscribe subjects; a literature that plays tricks on its readers (Harry Matthews, Vladimir Nabokov, Italo Calvino); a literature that empties itself of all the old pretensions, postures and impostures; a literature that seems exhausted and yet refuses to die—a LITERATURE OF EXHAUSTION, as John Barth called it in his 1968 seminal essay.

This crisis, however, did not reveal itself in our time with the advent of the New Fiction. It began to be felt in the middle of the nineteenth century—first as an existential crisis and then as an epistemological crisis. All the great thinkers and philosophers since the middle of the last century tried to offer means of solving the crisis—means of giving a sense of stability and continuity, and even a sense of permanence to a world that was falling apart: Darwin with the theory of evolution; the Positivists such as Ernest Renan and Auguste Comte with their affirmation of facts; Henri Bergson with the notion of intuitive thought based on movement and duration; Albert Einstein with his theory of relativity; Bertrand Russell with logical anatomism; the Phenomenologists with their insistence on beingness; and closer to us the Existentialists with their idea that existence precedes essence. Nietzsche was perhaps the only thinker to admit a rupture, and to proclaim a fragmentation of the world and of man's vision of the world.

Many artists and writers too attempted to preserve that vision of the world as a continuous, stable, and fixed succession of events. Realism affirmed logical and sequential continuity of experience, and Naturalism went even as far as demonstrating how man is predetermined by heredity, environment, and climate. However, in some cases, the great artists and writers of the end of the last century and of the twentieth century used this crisis as a source of inspiration. Consequently, fragmentation, incoherence, discontinuity, montage, collage, nonsense, chance happening, automatism, abstraction, stream of consciousness, and so on, became the governing elements of great art in the twentieth century.

Painting, through Impressionism, Cubism, and Constructivism blurred the lines of the real, and eventually reached total abstraction, that is to say the total erasing of reality. In poetry, symbolist poets such as Rimbaud, Lautréamont, Mallarmé (at least in France) dismantled conventional forms and poetic language, and after them the Dadaists, the Futurists, the Surrealists, and the Imagists, forced the entire logic of discursive language to fall apart. In fiction the progress (or perhaps one should say the process) was slower, because realism (the great imposture of illusionism) held fiction captive, except in a novel such a James Joyce's *Finnegans Wake* which outrageously blurred meaning by dislocating words and syntax to become a gigantic verbal edifice of unreadability.

In other words, at the same time as the world becomes more and more unintelligible, artists, poets, novelists realize that the real world is perhaps somewhere else—AILLEURS says the French poet Henri Michaux in a book by that title. And even if the world is not ELSEWHERE, it is a world no longer to be known, no longer to be expressed or represented, but to be imagined, to be invented anew.

The real world is now to be found in language, but not in the conventional, syntactical discourse that connected fiction to reality—the known world, the coherent, continuous, expressible world where, supposedly, words and things stuck to each other. On the contrary, the real world is now inside language, and can only be recreated by language, or what Rimbaud called *l'alchimie du verbe.* In our present world, words and things—*LES MOTS ET LES CHOSES,* as Michel Foucault so well demonstrated—no longer stick to each other, because language too is an autonomous reality.

Of course, not everyone is willing to accept this new conception of THE WORLD WITHIN THE WORD (as William Gass proposes in his collection of essays by that title), not all writers are willing to recognize a world without a preexisting meaning—a world of non-knowledge. The Positivists (and they are still very much present among us) want to stabilize knowledge, and consequently stabilize language at the same time. But this is a false premise. Logical Positivism wants to make sense out of the world, but faced with the limits of reality, it sets limits to language. "The limits of my world," wrote Wittgenstein, "are the limits of my language. What cannot be said cannot have meaning." Wittgenstein's statement is obviously meant as an anti-metaphysical proposition, but nonetheless it rationalizes language.

The New Fiction, on the contrary, rather than accepting the limitations of the possible, proposes no limits for language into the impossible, even if that language becomes contradictory or irrational. Indeed, the language of the New Fiction reaches beyond the rational, where the real and the imaginary, past and future, conscious and subconscious, and even life and death are no longer dichotomous. The New Fiction no longer opposes what is communicable to what is not communicable, what makes sense to what does not make sense, for there is as much value in making nonsense as there is in making sense. It is only a matter of direction.

Many characters in the New Fiction—or what I prefer to call the WORD-BEINGS of fiction—exist beyond reality as we know it, beyond life even, in a kind of absurd post-life condition, and in a totally illogical temporality and spatiality, free of all contradictions. As they wander in this liberated time and space (in novels such as *Cosmicomics* and *T/Zero*, by Calvino, or *How It Is* and *The Lost Ones*, by Beckett), these characters no longer need to rely on reason or memory to govern their activities since they exist only as beings made of words—the words of their fiction.

The impossible becomes possible in the New Fiction because language escapes analytical logic. It is a language which accepts and even indulges in contradictions; a language that plays with repetitions, permutations, neologisms, puns; a language that dislocates conventional syntax while designing a new typography, and in so doing renders the world even more unintelligible.

How, then, can the contemporary writer be *engagé*—socially and politically committed—since to be *engagé*, in the old Sartrean sense, there must be an intelligible and recognizable world, a world of stable and accepted values? To a great extent, the reason why Sartre's idea of a literary commitment failed is because he wanted all writers to agree on a system of moral, social, and political values, therefore denying the possibility of exploration and innovation into other systems. However, the one aspect of Sartre's thought that remains valid today is that of freedom, but a freedom which is not strictly and necessarily inclined socially, politically, or morally. It is above all, for today's writers, a linguistic freedom—a freedom of speech, one might say—a freedom to be able to say or write anything and everything, in any possible way. In this sense, this linguistic freedom to explore the impossible becomes as essential and as subversive as what Sartre proposed some forty-five years ago.

Of course, one can always argue that since there is nothing to know, then there is nothing to say. Or, as Robert Pinget once put it: "What is said is never said since one can always say it differently." And it is true that much of the New Fiction builds itself out of its own linguistic incapacity to express what cannot be expressed, and as such seems to make itself while unmaking itself. But since nothing is said, since nothing can be said, or since it can always be said differently, writers are now freed from what was denying them, what was negating them, and what was determining how they should write.

As far back as 1956, in a controversial essay entitled "A Future For the Novel," Alain Robbe-Grillet emphasized the absurdity and the impossibility of saying the world:

> *The world is neither significant nor absurd. It IS, quite simply. That, in*
> *any case, is the more remarkable thing about it. And suddenly, the obvi-*
> *ousness of this strikes us with irresistible force. All at once the whole*
> *splendid construction collapses; opening our eyes unexpectedly, we have*
> *experienced, once too often, the shock of this stubborn reality we were pre-*
> *tending to have mastered. Around us, defying the noisy pack of our ani-*
> *mistic or protective adjectives, things ARE THERE. Their surfaces are*
> *distinct and smooth, intact, neither suspiciously brilliant nor transpar-*
> *ent. All our literature has not yet succeeded in eroding their smallest*
> *corner, in flattening their slighest curve.*

Suddenly in this impossibility of saying the world appears the incredible possibility that everything can be said now, everything is on the
verge of being said **anew**. This explains why in much of New Fiction
one finds long meandering sentences, delirious verbal articulations,
repetitions, lists, questions without answers, factured parcels of words,
blank spaces where words should have been inscribed—an entire mechanism of linguistic montage and collage. It is as though the language of
fiction was taking an inventory of itself in an effort to grab things as
they are, to reassess the world, but without imposing a pre-established
signification upon it.

That is why much of the New Fiction often appears like a catalogue of
WHAT IS in the world, or **HOW IT IS** (as Beckett entitled one of his
novels), and no longer what we thought we **KNEW** of the world. There
is, therefore, behind this project an effort of sincerity—a search for a
new truth; a genuine effort to reinstate things, the world, and people in
their proper place—in a purified state. That, in my opinion, is also a
form of literary commitment. This extreme exigency of truth constitutes the honor and the purpose of the New Fiction at a time when literature (or what passes for literature on the best-sellers lists) remains all
too often an inconsequential network of illusions that perpetuates an
obsolete vision of the world.

This lucidity, this search for a new truth was already present in the
work of Artaud in the form of self-consciousness which forced him to
reply to those who reproached him for attaching too much importance
to language:

> *You don't see my thought . . . I know myself because I am my own spec-*
> *tator, I am Antonin Artaud's spectator . . . I am the one who has most*

clearly felt the bewildering confusion of his language in its relation with the world. I am the one who has best marked the moment of its most intimate, imperceptible shifts.

This questioning of one's existence and one's language becomes in the New Fiction its highest justification—if a justification is needed.

Reduced to non-sense, non-signification, non-knowledge, the world is no longer to be known or to be explained, it is to be **EXPERIENCED** as it is now recreated in the New Fiction, but no longer as an image (a realistic representation) or as an expression (vague feelings) of what we thought it was, but as a newly invented, newly discovered reality— a real fictitious reality.

2. SELF-REFLEXIVE FICTION
OR HOW TO GET RID OF IT

> . . . a satisfactory novel should be a self-evident sham to which the reader can regulate at will the degree of his credulity.
>
> —Flann O'Brien

Writing about self-reflexive fiction today, one is tempted to say, with a sigh of relief, at last **we got rid of it,** we have come to the end of this troublesome, irritating, exasperating form of narrative. But if self-reflexive fiction is finished, if we are finished with its gimmicks, its playfulness, its narcissism, its self-indulgence, nonetheless one should ask: What have we learned from it? In what sense has self-reflexiveness made the writing of fiction more interesting and perhaps even more potent? To what extent have the interrogations of self-reflexivity liberated the novel from certain obsolete conventions? And furthermore, to what extent has self-reflexiveness been incorporated into the fiction being written today, and as such has been rendered acceptable and even marketable?

While self-reflexive fiction was playing its tricks during the past three decades, insisting on drawing the reader into the confidence that the text was the only reality (not a mirror-image, but an image of itself), critics were quick to point out that there was nothing new in that, that it had all been done before, and inevitably sent the self-reflexive fictioneer (tail between his legs) back to *Tristram Shandy* or other such *preposterous* novels of the eighteenth century that had used and abused self-conscious and self-reflexive techniques, to good or bad purpose. And surely the history of the novel would be incomplete and incomprehensible without such novels as *Tristram Shandy* or Denis Diderot's *Jacques le Fataliste*, to mention only two of these so-called preposterous novels.

Certainly self-consciousness and self-reflexiveness are not new in the novel. They are not inventions of the 1960s or 1970s. All works of fiction are ultimately about themselves, about their process of coming into being and maintaining existence. That much any careful reader of fiction knows. Whether self-reflecting or simply reflecting, a work of fiction continually turns back on itself and draws the reader into itself as a text, as an ongoing narration, and before the reader knows what is happening, the text is telling him about itself. That is the fundamental truth of all fiction: it is always **implicitly** reflexive. The self-reflexive text, however, is one that **explicitly** concerns itself with the process of narration, with writing, with composition, and in so doing unveils the mechanism of its own making.

"In this matter of writing," Herman Melville states at the beginning of chapter 4 of *Billy Bud*, "resolve as one may to keep to the main road, some bypaths have an enticement not readily to be withstood. I am going to wander into such a bypath. If the reader will keep me company I shall be glad. At least we can promise ourselves that pleasure which is wickedly said to be in sinning, for a literary sin the divergence will be."

At various moments in the history of literature, the novel commits "the sin of divergence" whenever it needs to reaffirm its course; consequently self-reflexiveness which is a form of divergence (a digression from the story) becomes more explicit, more overt, and of course less subtle when the novel tries to extricate itself from an exhausted context in order to establish itself into a new context. But whatever it does, narration is always fascinated by the telling of the tale. This fascination of the novel with itself, which often turns to playfulness, begins with Cervantes' *Don Quixote*, it is present in the great work of Rabelais, *Gargantua and Pantagruel*, and it reaches its most explicit form in Laurence Sterne's *Tristram Shandy* where the author-narrator (that is to say the text itself) addresses the reader directly: "You must have a little patience. I have undertaken, you see, to write not only my life, but my opinions also."

This is explicit self-reflexiveness, and not all readers are willing to be "patient" while the author expresses his "opinions" or digresses away from the story. Impatient readers who want their fiction straight, without the author meddling with it, are quick to scream in frustration: *Skip the jazz and get on with the tale!*

If *Tristram Shandy* were an exception, an anomaly in the history of the novel, one would be tempted to ignore it, to skip it altogether, and get on with the tale. But along the way (from Cervantes to John Barth and beyond), one finds so many such splendid anomalies that one begins to wonder if in fact what is known as the tale, the conventional realistic tale is not itself the anomaly. However, as it progresses in time toward the modern novel and gradually rejects the mimetic pretensions of realism, self-reflexive fiction undergoes stages of sophistication. From *Tristram Shandy* to *Jacques le Fataliste*, though the two are almost contemporaneous, there is already a marked difference in the use of self-reflexiveness that affects the degree of realistic illusion. Though Sterne disrupts chronology with digressions and opinions, he anchors events firmly in time and place. His characters may be odd, but they are nonetheless saddled with everything necessary to make the reader believe in their actual existence in a somewhat real world. Diderot creates a space never before seen in the landscape of the novel: a timeless stage without scenery (not unlike that of the novels and plays of Samuel Beckett) where his characters function more as voices than as full-fledged personalities. Listening to Jacques and his Master talk, one always has the feeling that they are talking from inside a book rather than from reality. I know of no opening of a novel more engaging, more fascinating, and more self-reflexive than that of *Jacques le Fataliste*:

> *How did they meet? By chance, like everyone else. What were their names? What do you care. Where were they coming from? The nearest place. Where were they going? Does one really know where one is going? What were they saying? The master said nothing, and Jacques was saying that his captain was saying that everything that happens to us here on earth, good or bad, is written above.* [my translation]

It is certainly the playful self-reflexiveness of *Jacques le Fataliste* that makes of this novel the great fun book that it is, and this because Diderot not only meddles with the text but also offers the reader the possibility of participating in the fiction: "No, no. Of all the different abodes possible, which I have just enumerated, choose the one most appropriate to the present situation." Or even better, the author seduces the reader into the interplay of self-reflexiveness while pretending to be annoyed by the reader's impatience:

> *Where?—Where? Reader, you are of a rather cumbersome curiosity! By the Devil what does it matter? Even if I were to tell you that it was in Pontoise or in Saint-Germain, or in Notre-Dame de Lorette or Saint-Jacques de Compostelle, would you be better off? If you insist, I will tell you that they were going toward—yes, why not?—toward an immense castle, on the frontispiece of which was written: I belong to no one and I belong to everyone. You were here already before entering, and you will be here after departing.*

Clearly, Diderot, like Sterne and numerous other great novelists after him, understood that the novel is very much like the inscription on the frontispiece of the imaginary castle he invents on the spot: the novel belongs to no one and it belongs to everyone. We (as readers) were here before entering the book and we will still be here after closing it. This suggests that the process of reading a novel can be measured by the reader's willingness to engage—or let himself be engaged by—the self-reflexiveness of the text. Or as Flann O'Brien puts it in *At-Swim-Two-Birds* (a most outrageously self-reflexive novels): "... the reader can regulate at will the degree of his credulity." In this respect, the reader can be fascinated either by the tale only (which sends him back to his own reality) or by the telling of the tale (which keeps him inside the fiction).

One could go on quoting endlessly passages from great novels of the past that are self-reflexive either implicity or explicitly, for quite clearly most works of fiction are either self-conscious or self-reflexive, but in various degrees. However, what is not clear—and critics have often confused the terms—is the difference between self-consciousness and self-reflexiveness in a work of fiction. It seems essential at this point to try and clarify this question.

Self-consciousness, often irritating to the reader, establishes a conniving relation between author and reader, and is played above the text. As such it deals with the reading process. One could say that it is a public act that draws the reader into the privacy of the text, and therefore functions as a window that opens from outside into the text.

Self-reflexiveness, normally fascinating to the reader, establishes a playful relation between author and text, and therefore relates to the writing process. It is a private act, but one that makes itself public since it allows the reader to witness the interplay between author and creation. As such it functions like a mirror inside the text. Of course, self-conscious-ness and self-reflexiveness often intersect within the same novel and are not always distinguishable, for they both use the same tools—par-ody, irony, digression, playfulness—to demystify the illusionary aspects of the story.

The crucial difference between the kind of explicit self-reflexiveness one finds in the eighteenth-century novel, and that at work in the novel (the new novel) written in America during the 1960s and 1970s, is that the former reflected upon itself, unveiled its secrets, questioned its pos-sibilities in order to establish itself as a genre, as a respected literary genre, at a time when the novel was considered frivolous and even immoral, whereas the latter used similar techniques to extricate itself from the postures and impostures of realism and naturalism. In the first case it was a question of establishing a continuity for the novel, in the other it was a matter of creating a rupture in order to revive an "exhausted" genre—a genre that could no longer accommodate and express the extravagant notions of time and space of modern reality.

The publication in 1959 of *Naked Lunch* by William Burroughs marks the beginning of the new self-reflexive novel in America. Burroughs writes in *Naked Lunch*: "The world cannot be expressed, it can perhaps be indi-cated by mosaics of juxtaposition, like objects abandoned in a hotel room, defined by negatives and absence." And certainly, "negatives and absence" are the terms that best define the fiction written by the prominent new writers of the 1960s. William Burroughs, Flannery O'Connor, John Hawkes, Kurt Vonnegut Jr., John Barth, Richard Brauti-gan, Thomas Pynchon, Ishmael Reed, William Gass, William Gaddis, Jerzy Kosinski, Donald Barthelme, Robert Coover, and others form the first group, the first wave of self-reflexive (sometimes called postmod-ern) fictioneers who deliberately opposed the literary tendencies of what was then known as modernism. Already in the late 1950s, these writers began to challenge the terms that define modernist fiction— that is to say, the element of description and representation of social reality and its language, and the formalism (stream of consciousness, interior monologue, psychological depth, syncopated syntax) associ-ated with the inscribing of the subject into a fictional text. However, it cannot be said that these writers formed a unified movement for which a coherent theory could be formulated. On the contrary, the New Fiction was characterized by a multiplicity of individual voices that were defying critical ordering and rational interpretation (often to the despair of the critics).

In fact, it can be said of the New Fiction that it presented itself as a *mess*, and that therefore deliberate disorder, chaos, fragmentation, dislocation, discontuinity were its most striking aspects. But in this multiplicity of voices that echoed one another across the devastated landscape of fiction, there was a complicity of purpose that Jerome Klinkowitz loosely classified under the terms of *literary disruptions* (the title of his 1975 seminal study of what he called "Post-contemporary Fiction").

It is true that this New Fiction created a disruptive complicity as it undermined the modernist tradition and rejected its mimetic function. While reflecting upon itself, upon its own means and possibilities, the New Novel offered itself as a collection of fragments, as a puzzling catalogue of lists, as a montage or collage of disparate elements. This tendency toward bringing together the incongruous and even the incompatible opposed the type of fiction based on metaphoric and symbolic representation of reality. Consequently the New Novel was viewed, by most critics, as being caught between paranoia and schizophrenia, as though hesitating between conjunction and disjunction, and thus unable to render itself coherent and logical, unable to probe below the surface. What was not clearly understood, however, is that this fiction of surfaces (as it was called) deliberately refused to fall into the old psychological trap of modernism.

If the traditional novel continued to describe and explain reality in an effort to give that reality a certain moral and even spiritual order, based on the obsolete formulas of realism and naturalism, the New Fiction (created on the margin of the literary establishment) sought to show the form rather than the content of American reality. It tried to render concrete and even visual in its language, in its typography and topology, the disorder, the chaos, the violence, the incongruity, but also the energy and vitality, of American reality. In this sense, the New Fiction was closer to the truth of America than the old ponderous and realistic novel of the 1950s. To achieve its aims, the New Fiction brought together fragments of reality, remnants and detritus, or what Donald Barthelme called "the American dreck," and what Gilbert Sorrentino defines as "the imaginative qualities of actual things" (which happens to be the title of one of his more self-reflexive novels).

Whereas modernist literature manipulated ancient myths and stable symbols, the New Fiction confronted and exploded contemporary clichés. In this sense there was a rupture with the modernist tradition. But beyond this literary and formalistic rupture, which critics have been discussing and analyzing for quite some time now, there is another form of rupture relevant to the understanding of the self-reflexive novel that has become visible in retrospect, and that is the rupture that occurred during the 1960s between the official discourse and the subject. By official discourse I mean that of the State, that of the Establishment, and by subject the individual who receives the official discourse whether it is political, social, economic, or cultural.

The first signs of this rupture appeared around 1960, and corresponded to some degree to the emergence of the New Fiction. From the end of World War II to the election of John F. Kennedy (in 1960) there was in America a kind of unequivocal relation between individual desires and the mechanism through which the State expressed itself. By State it must be understood that I mean not only the government but all the institutions that make America, including of course the university as well as the publishing industry.

The 1950s, on the surface at any rate, were a period of social and economic optimism. The American economy was booming as a follow-up to the war, resulting in a great demand for a better standard of living (that is to say a great demand for objects: cars, televisions, washing machines, houses, etc.—many of these quickly becoming status symbols). At the same time America was asserting its position of strength throughout the world, making its political but also cultural impact felt. The key term in public life was the achievement of **success**.

The 1950s, in other words, were a period of **valorization** and **symbolization** of the American way of life and the American reality. However, underlying this economic and spiritual boom was a sense of absurdity to the whole undertaking—a sense of the absurd left over from Existentialism, which had come to America from across the Atlantic and was now reflected in such wartime and postwar novels as Saul Bellow's *Dangling Man* (1944), John Hawkes's *The Cannibal* (1949), and even in John Barth's early novels, *The Floating Opera* (1956) and *The End of the Road* (1958).

The American writers of the 1950s were known as "the silent generation," not because they had nothing to say, or said nothing, but rather because they, to a great extent, expressed in their work a silent agreement with the official political, moral, and social attitudes of the State. Yet, in most of the novels published during that decade (one thinks of the novels of Saul Bellow, Norman Mailer, J. D. Salinger, Herman Wouk, Bernard Malamud, William Styron, and many others), a sense of the absurd permeated the texts even though it never really surfaced. It was only with *Catch 22* by Joseph Heller, published in 1961, that the absurdity of World War II exploded into the open in a self-reflexive manner. In general, however, the fiction of the 1950s (except for the stir created by the Beat Generation, perhaps more over personalities than literary works) offered a somewhat optimistic and moralistic resolution to contemporary problems.

By the time President Kennedy took office, America was ready to receive the kind of electrifying and electronic image he projected through the mass media and that quickly lodged itself in the American consciousness. And it is that image, that sublimated image, especially when it appeared on television, that structured the subject (the American people). The message and the image that Kennedy presented offered themselves as the defenders of a rational discourse that had finally triumphed over the irrational discourse that had led to Nazi and Fascist politics, and that was then openly shaping Communist ideology and action in Budapest in 1956, in Cuba in 1962, and in other parts of the world. In other words, the official message and image of the 1950s and early 1960s seemed good, honest, truthful, and tough when necessary. Thus when Kennedy smiled that meant that he was happy, and America was happy. When he spoke in a grave tone of voice and announced that the country could be destroyed in an atomic blast coming from Cuba, the entire nation changed mood. There existed then an element of mutual trust between the official discourse and the subject, just as there existed an element of trust on the part of the readers for the fiction written at that time. That discourse presented itself as a personal friend, and so did, in fact, much of the fiction written immediately after World War II—a fiction of easy moral and social resolutions, as for instance Herman Wouk's *Marjorie Morningstar* or Norman Mailer's *The Deer Park*, both published in 1955 with great popular success. This is why the assassination of John F. Kennedy (public and televised) had such a traumatic impact on the American consciousness.

Suddenly things were not as good as they appeared. Suddenly the American people were doubting the very reality of the events they were witnessing, especially on television. It took certain blunders of the John-son administration, and subsequently the manipulations and lies of the Nixon administration, and of course the Vietnam War, and the Water-gate debacle to awaken America from its mass media state of illusion and optimism. Suddenly there was a general distrust of the official dis-course whether spoken, written, or televised. For indeed, if the content of history can be manipulated by the mass media, if television and newspapers can falsify or justify historical facts, then the unequivocal relation between the real and the imaginary disappear. The clear line that separates fact from fiction is blurred. Consequently, historical events must be doubted, reviewed, reexamined, especially recent events as presented, or rather as RE-presented to us by the mass media and by fiction.

By the end of the Watergate crisis, all the official versions dealing with the Cold War, the McCarty era, the Korean War (never officially desig-nated as a war), CIA activities in various parts of the world, the Vietnam War of course, and so on are being mistrusted, questioned, and chal-lenged not only in political writing, not only in the New Journalism that emerges as a new mode of writing in the 1960s as a result of the blurring of fact and fiction, but also in the novel as it establishes a new relation with reality and with history, a relation based on doubt.

The self-reflexive novel that takes shape during the 1960s in a way fills the linguistic gap created by the disarticulation of the official discourse in its relation with the individual. It places into the open, in order to challenge it, the question of representation in fiction, especially now that the line between the real and the imaginary has been erased. When the historical discourse is falsified as language, referential coherence collapses and becomes irrelevant. It is this idea that sets off the first wave of self-reflexiveness in the novel (between 1960 and 1968) when it questions but also mocks and parodies, with *black humor*, the official discourse, and even more so the historical discourse of America.

Though the syntax remains normative, discursive, and even linear, and the narrative metonymic, nonetheless the novels written during that period are audacious in terms of their subject matter, and of what can be called their *irrealism*. Most of these novels continue to perform on the principle that storytelling cannot be totally eliminated, but the narra-tive becomes fragmented, discontinuous, and ironic, as if it had lost con-trol in relation to the electronic mirror where life (and death in many cases) is decided by technological absurdity. As presented in these novels, history and the subject are two faces of an immense farce, a collective farce, and the text simply shows the absurd relation between the two.

In the novel of the 1960s, where official history is mixed with the picaresque and burlesque adventures of the individual, where the characters have no other substance than their fictitious personalities since they exist only as verbal beings, the author denounces the symbolic strata that shape history and the individual. Most of these novels propose nothing, they only illustrate the fact that reality is but a fraudulent verbal network, for to replace one reality with another is a senseless undertaking, because one merely substitutes one symbolic system for another, one set of illusions for another. Therefore, all periods of American history are now being remade, replayed self-reflexively, as well as ironically in these parody-novels that often use the mass media as a backdrop, as for instance in the early fiction of Kurt Vonnegut Jr., Robert Coover, Donald Barthelme, Ishmael Reed, and Richard Brautigan.

The Sotweed Factor (1960) by John Barth retells the history of the colonial period in an inverted direction: no longer the traditional picaresque and burlesque adventures of the European who comes to the New World to seek his fortune, but the American who returns to the Old World to retrace his confused origin and unmake his fortune, and in the process demystifies American history and its language. A Confederate General from Big Sur (1964) by Richard Brautigan neutralizes the Civil War, and thus negates its dramatic and traumatic impact in order to expose its absurdity. Robert Coover in The Origin of the Brunists (1965) makes a mockery of religious cults in America by using a complex plot founded upon a prior mythic and historical source that eventually releases an antiformal revelation; by abusing a familiar form, Coover undercuts the hold that the content of this form has on people. Ishmael Reed in The Free-Lance Pallbearers (1967), but especially in Mumbo Jumbo (1972) and Flight to Canada (1976), retells in satirical terms the history of slavery in America; it is as though the old classic, Uncle Tom's Cabin, is being reshuffled and presented from a reversed point of view. However, it is particularly World War II and the Cold War, the events that shaped the very life of this generation of writers, that become the main targets of their parody-novels.

Most novels written during the 1950s glorified World War II as a good war, a necessary war, and even as a great adventure, in spite of its tragic aspects. One thinks, for instance, of such novels as *From Here to Eternity* (James Jones), *The Young Lions* (Irwin Shaw), *The Naked and the Dead* (Norman Mailer), *The Caine Mutiny* (Herman Wouk), and so many other war-inspired novels. This type of fiction is now being demystified and undercut by the parody and irony of the new novel. *Catch 22* is, of course, the most striking example, but such novels as *V* (1963) by Thomas Pynchon, *Mother Night* (1961) and especially *Slaughterhouse Five* (1966) by Kurt Vonnegut Jr., *The Painted Bird* (1965) by Jerzy Kosinski, and *Giles Goat-Boy* (1966) by John Barth also mock recent American history to the point of reducing it to an absurd farce.

What these novels are doing is questioning the official version of historical events. In most cases, the protagonists seem to be searching for a missing coherence in their lives and in their actions. Most of these authors are intent on revising their position and their views in relation to the events that they themselves helped shape, and they do so self-reflexively in the dual role of narrator and protagonist of their own fiction. Often they cannot decide (as the grandiose disembodied figure of Samuel Beckett's *The Unnamable*—a model for many novels of the 1960s—states himself) whether they are "the teller or the told."

In *Slaughterhouse Five*, the author himself (under his own name, Kurt Vonnegut) as the narrator-protagonist of the story returns to the place where he participated in the war (in this case Dresden), but not to remember how it was, not to relive nostalgically what he did, not to experience again the feeling of the great adventure, but to rethink, revise his vision of that tragic and absurd moment. In other words, Kurt Vonnegut does not simply write a novel to remember for us "*how it was in the war,*" he does not offer to the reader memories or souvenirs of the war, but instead he confronts and even implicates that reader with self-reflexive visions and revisions of the events in which the author participated, thus denouncing in the process the absurdity of these events as well as the vehicle through which they were related.

The fundamental rule of these self-reflexive narratives is the absurd and the arbitrary. The fictional machine seems to turn into a void, but not without cringing irony and black humor. At the end of these intricate stories there is no real message, no order, no easy resolution, no pseudomoral statement, only a text that offers itself as a kind of nonsense delirium that, to a great extent, reflects the nonsense of historical events and the delirium of the language recounting these events.

Though the same ironic mood is maintained in much of the fiction written after 1968 through the 1970s, suddenly a more experimental and innovative form of writing appears. The language of fiction undergoes radical changes: the syntax is pulverized, in some cases reaching into visual concreteness on the pages, as in such works as Steve Katz's *The Exagggerations of Peter Prince* (with three *g*'s—1968), Madeline Gins's *World Rain* (1969), or William Gass's *Willie Master's Lonesome Wife* (1971). The language of fiction now takes on the form of what Ihab Hassan has called (in reference to my own novel *Double or Nothing* [1971]) "visual self-reflexive exuberance . . . and typographical laughter" as the book itself becomes a performance where the narrative constantly deviates from linearity and sequential logic into a spiraling mode of digressions, or what has been called "the leap-frog technique."

In some of these novels, such as *Gravity's Rainbow* (1973) by Thomas Pynchon, or *The Public Burning* (1977) by Robert Coover, the subject matter remains a parody of World War II or the Cold War: Pynchon creates a gigantic and grotesquely confused, deliberately confused picture of the war in England, while Coover recounts in his own mocking and carnavalesque manner the trial of the Rosenbergs with Richard Nixon as the central, pathetic, and comic figure. However, in these novels that appear after 1968, the element of parody is gradually replaced by pure irony and explicit self-reflexiveness, which release new energies into the language of fiction. Moreover, the blasphemous humor and the playfulness of these novels displace not only the somber black humor of the early postmodern novels but especially the seriousness of the intellectual and often moralistic novels of the 1950s, in particular that of the Jewish novel and that of the Southern novel. The heavy morality of the Jewish novel which took shape during the 1950s, whose psychologically insecure hero carried on his shoulder the entire burder of truth (the traumatic truth learned during the war) and of guilt, is now exploded in the late 1960s. The typical Jewish novel of Saul Bellow, Isaac Bashevis Singer, Bernard Malamud, Herbert Gold, and to some extent Norman Mailer, which imposed on its characters (and its readers too) a gloomy sense of responsibility and culpability, is demystified by such novels as Philip Roth's *Portnoy's Complaint* (1969), or in a much more experimental and playful manner, by Ronald Sukenick in his novel *Up* (1968), by Jonathan Baumbach in *Reruns* (1974), or in my own novel *Take It or Leave It* (1976).

The Jewish novel, and similarly the Southern novel—those literary discourses of moral responsibility and of silent agreement with the official discourse of the State—seem as hollow today as the historical discourse out of which they took shape. These novels are transformed in the late 1960s and in the 1970s by the use of humor and irony, but above all by the introduction of explicit sexuality into the text whereby the protagonists become (as in the case of Portnoy) outrageous libidinal figures who mock by their actions and their language the social, ethnic, regional, and moral tradition within which they function. The same is also true of the black novel. Ralph Ellison's *Invisible Man* (1952), Richard Wright's *Native Son* (1953), and even James Baldwin's *Another Country* (1962), though they remain powerful novels, are nonetheless radically transformed in the fiction of Ishmael Reed, Clarence Major, Charles Johnson, John Edgar Wideman, four of the more experimental and self-reflexive black novelists of the last three decades.

As for the great mythic dramas of the South, so beautifully orchestrated by William Faulkner, and perpetuated in a similar vein by William Styron in *Lie Down in Darkness* (1951), or Walker Percy in *The Moviegoes* (1962), these are now reduced to a kind of comic strip fiction in Richard Brautigan's novels and especially in the stories of Flannery O'Connor. The Civil War, that great historical discourse so typically American, which persisted to shape Southern fiction and produced somber, serious characters who existed within sophisticated dramatic situations, such as those created by Faulkner, the Civil War is no longer the traumatic event which cornered its subjects into an eternal Oedipus complex and an incestuous social and familial existence. In Flannery O'Connor's fiction, the Civil War is barely a memory in the minds of middle-class people who are shaped by the clichés of the language they use. Though still writing within the formulas of modernism, in such fine books as *A Good Man Is Hard to Find* (1955) and *The Violent Bear It Away* (1960), Flannery O'Connor already announces the principles of self-reflexive fiction in her fragmented narratives, and her subtle use of clichés, but especially in the way she reduces the seriousness of the Southern novel to a mocking casualness. For it is certainly fragmented narrative, the use, or rather the abuse of clichés, and the burlesque enunciation of social and historical events that best characterize the new fiction written in America during the 1970s, as if it were now functioning on the brink of constant disaster.

The work of Donald Barthelme, especially in his shorter stories, typifies this kind of fiction which accepts the degradation of language and its trashy condition. Thus it is the disarticulation of language, and the self-reflexivity of the text that prevent the story to take shape in a linear and coherent fashion. It is in this deliberate refusal to render itself coherent and accessible that the self-reflexive fiction of the 1970s becomes more radical and innovative.

If William Burroughs' *Naked Lunch*, as early as 1959, implied the initial rupture between the individual and the structuring discourse of the State, his trilogy—*The Soft Machine* (1961), *The Ticket that Exploded* (1962), and *Nova Express* (1964)—went further than most of the early postmodern texts in proposing a radical linguistic experience instead of a mere linear satire of history. For Burroughs, the text itself is never innocent, and therefore a friendly accommodating relationship between author and reader, between the writing subject and the reading subject is not to be sought. The literary discourse and the words that make that discourse are biological enemies, for these are the fundamental elements of representation of a human being and of his place in history.

The historical and political parody-novels of the early 1960s (those of Heller, Barth, Pynchon, Reed, etc.) described a world where imaginary beings wandered aimlessly in a baroque landscape, and where narrative possibilities were infinite. What these were suggesting is that the central machine, the giant computer ("The mighty WESTCAC," of John Barth's *Giles Goat-Boy*) that controls the relation between images and desire, between the real and the imaginary, was now in a perpetual state of disorder and disarray. But there were no real political implications in the work of these writers, unless parody as such can be viewed as a political gesture.

The political nature of William Burroughs's fiction goes beyond mere satire or parody because he is not satisfied to simply mock history, or to show the absurdity of the world for the sake of intelligence or the sake of art. He wants to denounce the very mechanism that creates evil and injustice in the world. Since evil is deeply rooted in human flesh and in human desire, and reveals itself in language, the controlling machine perpetuates what Burroughs calls "the virus-word," which produces the identification of desire through linguistic fixation.

Though using more radical and even more reductive techniques, the New Fiction writers who emerge after 1968 work in the same direction as William Burroughs. Their fiction may not be as political as his, but nonetheless it is subversive, for these writers are less interested in parodying the world or mocking history than transforming the language through which the world and history are represented. Rather than reducing history and the individual who performs in history to a kind of absurd comic strip, as the early postmodernists did, the second wave of writers use experimental forms to disarticulate language from the inside. They achieve this especially through explicit self-reflexiveness that liberates the fiction from illusionism and even from fictionality. Many novels written in the 1970s read more like essays than pure fiction, or what I call **critifiction**: a kind of narrative that contains its own theory and even its own criticism.

I have already mentioned Ronald sukenick whose first novel *Up* (1968) announced this new trend. In 1969, Sukenick published a brilliant collection of stories appropriately entitled *The Death of the Novel and Other Stories*, followed by the novel *Out* (1973), then in 1976 another curiously entitled novel *98.6*, in 1980 *Long Talking Bad Conditions Blues*, in 1986 *The Endless Short-Story*, and the same year *Blown Away* an outrageous self-reflexive satire of Hollywood. Sukenick's body of fiction exemplifies the way language and narrative structures are exploded in the fiction of the 1970s. He constructs his fiction on the principle of a fundamental and sustained opposition: the construction of a fictional illusion and the laying bare of that illusion. In other words, he creates a fiction and simultaneously makes a statement about the creation of that fiction. The two processes are held together in a formal tension that breaks down the distinction between fact and fiction, between fiction and criticism, between imagination and reflection, and as a result the concepts of creation and interpretation merge into a new type of discourse—a critifictional discourse. To achieve this, Ronald Sukenick (the author) is always present in his fiction (usually under his own name) but as a fictional/mythical figure: an author-narrator-critic-theoretician-protagonist.

Walter Abish, Steve Katz, George Chambers, Gilbert Sorrentino, Madeline Gins, Kenneth Gangemi, Michael Stephens, Clarence Major, Ursule Molinaro (and I suppose I should place my name among these) are writers of the 1970s who work in a vein similar to that of Ronald Sukenick. What differentiates this group from the early postmodernists is a more daring, a more radical use of language, but also a total rejection of traditional forms of narrative, and especially of mimetic realism and mimetic pretension. One could say that the new fiction of the 1970s evolved out of the need to escape the manipulation of language as a trap in its relation to reality and history, in order to do so it conceptualized a new type of discourse that constantly draws attention to itself: its own medium, its own process of fiction-making.

As of 1968, fiction offers texts that are analogous to language, texts that reflect upon their own movement, and that function between social reality and subjectivity in order to undermine the illusory relationship between the two. It is no longer a question of representing or explaining or justifying American reality, but a question of denouncing the vehicle that expressed and represented that reality: discursive language and the traditional form of the novel. In other words, the New Fiction writers confront their own writing, insert themselves inside their own texts in order to question the very act of using language to write fiction, even at the risk of alienating the reader.

The spirals of self-reflexiveness have often been accused of being unhealthy both for the writer and for the reader. In a world where daily reality offers fantasies and phantasms that go beyond those the writer can invent, certain critics have deplored the fact that writers abandon realism, desert the facts of history, and mock the idea of credibility and truth in order to indulge in narcissistic games that prevent the reader from identifying with the characters of the fiction. Self-reflexive writers have been attacked for turning their backs on social consciousness and political commitment, for refusing to explain reality, for refusing to pretend any longer that reality is equivalent to truth, and therefore failing to render reality coherent and rational. Of course, such arguments fail to understand that perhaps there are deeper reasons—reasons of psychological and even political order—that force the new writers to abandon the tradition of realism. Such arguments fail to recognize that the techniques of parody, irony, introspection, self-reflexiveness directly challenge the oppressive forces of social and literary authorities.

Confronting the fiasco of recent historical events, the New Novelists ("chaos-drunk writers," as Gerald Graff calls them) offer a new idea of history: since civilization has become fraudulent, since it has turned into an enormous lie, it is important to examine its deceptions, its ruins, its clichés—"the mess of civilization and culture," as Samuel Beckett once put it. But above all it is important to examine and denounce the language that continues to perpetuate lies and illusions. Therefore, for the self-reflexive writers who see culture, or rather the discourse produced by culture, as a mystification, it becomes crucial to empty language of its symbolic power. It is in this sense that the New Fiction writers are involved in an act of *disruptive complicity* as they confront the mess of reality, or what I called elsewhere "the unreality of reality."

Of course the game is never innocent, the farce never totally gratuitous. Everything happens in the New Fiction as if the world suddenly confronted the dilemma of having to choose between renouncing the rationality of language or renouncing individual desires. The New Novelists abandon the search for stable points of reference in reality and in history, abandon also the purely formalistic temptation that dominated literature before World War II and ultimately led to Jame Joyce's *Finnegans Wake*, certainly the greatest unreadable linguistic tour de force ever written. Instead the new writers have chosen the play of irrationality, the free play of language over discursive coherence and formalistic unity. Gradually then the stable syntax and the readable irony of the early parody-novels of the 1960s are disintegrated into a form of deliberate unreadability not unlike that of *Finnegans Wake*, not simply for aesthetic reason, however, but for subversive reasons.

On first reading, such novels as George Chambers's The *Bonnyclabber* (1972), Walter Abish's *Alphabetical Africa* (1974), Gilbert Sorrentino's *Mulligan Stew* (1979), Ronald Sukenick's *Long Talking Bad Conditions Blues*, Clarence Major's *Emergency Exit* (1979), and my own novel *The Voice in the Closet* (1979) are books that may be declared exasperating and unreadable because of their extreme self-reflexiveness and their typographical "exuberance," yet that so-called unreadability raises fundamental questions about the role of fiction today. Basically it exposes the fixation of desires in language. By rendering language seemingly incoherent, irrational, illogical, and even meaningless, these works of fiction negate the symbolic power of language while proposing at the same time a purification of that language so that it can no longer structure or even enslave the individual into a sociohistorical scenario prepared in advance and replayed by the official discourse on television, in the mass media, in the political arena, and in literature.

"The world cannot be expressed, it can only be indicated by mosaics of juxtaposition, like objects abandoned in a hotel room, defined by negatives and absence." It is worth quoting again this passage from *Naked Lunch*. In many ways, the experimental American novel of the last three decades seems to have verified and asserted the truth of this statement. For indeed by rendering language seemingly irrational, and even unreadable in some instances, the New Fiction writers have also neutralized the fiasco of reality and the imposture of history. By confronting the unreality of reality, they have come closer to the truth of the world today, just as Laurence Sterne and Denis Diderot did in their own time.

3. SURFICTION:
A POSTMODERN POSITION

Now some people might say that the situation of fiction today is not very encouraging, but one must reply that it is not meant to encourage those who say that!
—Raymond Federman

Writing about fiction today, one could begin with the usual clichés: the novel is dead; writing fiction is no longer possible nor necessary because **real** fiction happens, everyday, in the streets of our cities, in the spectacular hijacking of planes, in space, on the Moon, in the Middle-East, in China, in Eastern Europe, and of course on television (especially during the news broadcasts); fiction has become obsolete and irrelevant because life has become much more interesting, much more dramatic, much more intriguing and incredible than what the dying novel can possibly offer.

And one could go on saying that writing fiction is now impossible (as many theoreticians and practitioners of fiction have demonstrated lately) because all the possibilities of fiction have been used up, abused, exhausted, and therefore all that is left, to the one who still insists on writing fiction, is to repeat (page after page, *ad nauseam*) that there is nothing to write about, nothing with which to write, and thus simply continue to write that there is nothing to write (as for instance the so-called *Nouveau Roman* in France has been doing for the past forty years).

Indeed, such works of non-fiction as Truman Capote's *In Cold Blood*, or Norman Mailer's *The Day Kennedy Was Shot* and *Armies of the Night*, or Hunter Thompson's *Fear and Loathing in Las Vegas,* and all those books written recently about terrorism, drug trafficking, violence, financial sucess or financial disaster, political scandals, and all those autobiographies written by people who supposedly have experienced **real life** in the streets of our cities, in the ghettos, in the jails, in the political arena, on the stock-markets of the world, are possibly better fictions thant the foolish and vacuous stories (love stories, murder stories, spy stories, adventure stories, sexual deviate stories, the rich and the famous stories, and so on) the novel—the commercial novel that is—is still trying to peddle and make us believe.

Yes, one could start this way, and simply give up on fiction, abandon the novel forever. For as Samuel Beckett once said: "It is easy to talk about being unable, whereas in reality nothing is more difficult."

Well, I propose that the novel is far from being dead (and I mean now the traditional novel—that moribund novel that became moribund the day it was conceived, some four hundred years ago when Cervantes wrote *Don Quixote*). I propose that, in fact, this type of novel is still very much alive—very **healthy** and very **wealthy** too. I know many novelists who can brag that their latest book has brought them one million dollars, two million dollars, or more. James Michener, Harold Robbins, Judith Krantz are only three of the many second-rate rich novelists who should be mentioned. No, the commercial novel is not dead; it is quite prosperous in some parts of the world.

But if we are to talk **seriously** about fiction—**serious** fiction—this is not the kind of writers and the kind of fiction I am interested in. The kind of fiction I am interested in is that fiction that those who control the literary establishment (publishers, editors, agents, reviewers, booksellers, etc.) brush aside because it does not conform to **their** notions of what fiction should be, or how it should be written, and consequently has no value (commercial that is) for the common reader. And the easiest way for these people to brush aside that kind of fiction is to label it, quickly and bluntly, as **experimental.**

Everything that does not fall into the category of **successful fiction** (commercially that is), or what Jean-Paul Sartre once called "*la littérature alimentaire*" (nutritious literature), everything that is found "unreadable for our readers" (that's the way publishers and editors speak— but who gave them the right to decide what is **readable** or **valuable** for the readers?) is immediately relegated to the domain of experimentation—a safe and useless place.

Personally I do not believe that a fiction writer with the least amount of self-respect and integrity, and who believes in what he is doing, ever says to himself: "I am now going to write an experimental novel." Others say that about his work. It is the middleman, the procurer of literature (the failed novelist turned editor or journalist) who gives that label **EXPERIMENTAL** to what is unusual, difficult, innovative, provocative, intellectually challenging, and even original. In fact, true experiments (as in the sciences) never reach, or at least should never reach the printed page. A novel is always a form of experiment, and therefore becomes an experience. After all the two terms were synonymous at one time. Fiction is called experimental out of incomprehension and despair. It is those who are unwilling to give to a novel what it demands intellectually that declares that novel experimental. Samuel Beckett's novels are not experimental—no!—it is the only way he could write them; Jorge Luis Borges' stories are not experimental; Italo Calvino's fiction is not experimental; or going back in time to James Joyce or Franz Kafka, their fiction is not experimental (even though it was called that when it first appeared and is still called that by those who cannot accept what departs from the norm or refuses to submit to simple-mindedness). All these writers created successful and accomplished works of art that function on their own terms rather than on a set of predetermined rules.

And so, for me, the only fiction that still means something today is the kind of fiction that tries to explore the possibilities of fiction beyond its own limitations; the kind of fiction that challenges the tradition that governs it; the kind of fiction that constantly renews our faith in man's intelligence and imagination rather than man's distorted view of reality; the kind of fiction that reveals man's playful irrationality rather than his righteous rationality.

This I call **SURFICTION**. However, not because it imitates reality, but because it exposes the fictionality of reality. Just as the Surrealists called that level of man's experience that functions in the subconscious **SURREALITY**, I call that level of man's activity that reveals life as a fiction **SURFICTION**. In this sense there is some truth in the cliché that claims that "life imitates fiction," or that "life is like fiction," but not because of what is happening in the streets of our cities, but because reality as such does not exist, or rather exists only in its fictionalized version, that is to say in the language that describes it.

The experiences of life gain meaning only in their recounted form, in their verbalized versions, or as Louis-Ferdinand Céline stated, some years ago, in answer to those who claimed that his novels were barely disguised autobiographies: "Life, also, is fiction . . . and a biography is something one invents afterwards."

But in what sense is life fiction? To live is to understand that one lives, and fiction is above all an effort to apprehend and comprehend human existence played on the level of words, and only on the level of words. Or as Roland Barthes once put it: "The book creates meaning, and meaning creates life." In other words, fiction is made of understanding which for most of us means primarily words—only words (spoken or written). Therefore, if one admits from the start (at least to oneself) that no meaning precedes language, but that language creates meaning as it goes along, that is to say as it is used (spoken or written), as it progresses, then writing (fiction especially) will be a mere process of letting language do its tricks.

To write, then, is to **PRODUCE** meaning, and not **REPRODUCE** a pre-existing meaning. To write is to **PROGRESS**, and not **REMAIN** subjected (by habit or reflexes) to the meaning that supposedly precedes language. As such fiction can no longer be reality, or an imitation of reality, or a representation of reality, or even a re-creation of reality; it can only be itself a reality—an autonomous reality whose only relation to the real world is to improve that world. To create fiction today is, in fact, to transform reality, and to some extent even abolish reality, and especially abolish the notion that reality is truth.

Therefore, rather than serving as a mirror or redoubling on itself, fiction adds itself to the world thus creating a meaningful relation that did not previously exist. Though fiction is often viewed as an artifice, it is not artificial. To write fiction today is before all an effort to create a **DIFFER-ENCE**, and not to pretend that fiction is the same thing as reality. The traditional realistic novel was a representation of the **SAME**. Surfiction will be a presentation of difference—a liberation of what is different.

Defining the contemporary discourse, Michel Foucault wrote some twenty years ago: "In order to liberate difference we must have a contradictory thought, free of dialectic, free of negation. A thought that says yes to divergence; an affirmative thought, whose instrument is disjunction; a thought of the multiple; a thought that does not obey a scholarly model, but that addresses insoluble problems within a play of repetition."

Though Michel Foucault was only trying to define how the contemporary historical or philosophical discourse ought to function, his definition seems applicable to the surfictional discourse as well. Far from being the incomplete and blurred image of an **IDEA** which, from time immemorial, held some absolute answer, the problem of fiction today is to affirm an **IDEA** in which the question never ceases to be displaced toward another question. What is the answer to this question? The problem itself. How to solve this problem? By constantly displacing the question. That, in effect, is how Surfiction functions.

Displacement, difference, and repetition, these are the givens of Surfiction, and no longer faithful imitation and truthful representation. Consequently, in the fiction of today and tomorrow, all distinctions between the real and the imaginary, between the conscious and the subconscious, between the past and the present, between truth and untruth will be abolished. All forms of duplicity will disappear. And above all, all forms of duality will be negated—yes, especially duality: that double-headed monster which for centuries subjected us to a system of ethical and aesthetical values based on the principles of good and bad, true and false, beautiful and ugly.

Surfiction will not be judged on such principles. It will neither be good nor bad, true nor false, beautiful nor ugly. It will simply **BE**, and its primary purpose will be to unmask its own fictionality, to expose the metaphor of its own fraudulence and simulacrum, and not pretend any longer to pass for reality, for truth, or for beauty.

As a result, Surfiction will no longer be regarded as a mirror of life, as a pseudorealistic document that informs us about life, nor will it be judged on the basis of its social, moral, psychological, metaphysical, or commercial value, but only on the basis of what it is and what it does as an autonomous art form in its own right—just as poetry, music or the plastic arts are autonomous.

These preliminary remarks serve as an introduction to four propositions I would now like to make for the present-future of fiction. These are but an arbitrary starting point for the possibilities of a New Fiction. Other positions and other propositions are possible. My propositions will be dogmatic, but that's how it should be, because this text is in fact a manifesto for Surfiction, and as such it can only be dogmatic. One accepts or rejects a manifesto in its entirety, but one cannot argue with it. That is the ironic idea inscribed in the epigraph to this text (quoted from one of my surfictional novels) which I want to reaffirm in order to discourage those who will disagree with me: "Now some people might say that the situation of fiction today is not very encouraging but one must reply that it is not meant to encourage those who say that!"

PROPOSITION ONE—THE READING OF FICTION

The very act of reading a book, starting at the top of the first page, and moving from left to right, top to bottom, page after page to the end in a consecutive prearranged manner has become *restrictive and boring*. Indeed, any intelligent reader should feel frustrated and restricted within that preordained system of reading.

Therefore, the whole traditional, conventional, fixed, and boring method of reading a book must be questioned, challenged, and demolished. And it is the writer (and not modern printing technology alone) who must, through innovations in the writing itself—in the typography of the text and the topography of the book—renew our system of reading.

All the rules and principles of printing and bookmaking must be forced to change as a result of the changes in the writing (or the telling) of a story in order to give the reader a sense of free participation in the writing/reading process, in order to give the reader an element of choice (active choice) in the ordering of the discourse and the discovery of its meaning.

Thus the very concept of syntax must be transformed. Syntax, traditionally, is the unity, the continuity of words, the law that dominates them. Syntax reduces the multiplicity of words and controls their energy and their violence. It fixes words into a place, a space, and pre-scribes an order to them. It prevents words from wandering. Even if it is hidden, syntax always reigns on the horizon of words which buckle under its mute exigency.

Therefore, words, sentences, paragraphs (and of course the punctua-tion) and their position on the page and in the book must be rethought and rewritten so that new ways (multiple and simultaneous ways) of reading these can be created. And even the typographical design of the pages and the numbering of these pages must be reinvented. The space itself in which writing takes place must be transformed. That space—the page, but also the book made of pages—must acquire new dimensions, new shapes, new relations in order to accommodate the new writing. Pages no longer need to be the same uniform rectangular size, and books no longer need to be rectangular boxes. It is within this trans-formed topography of writing, from this new **paginal syntax** rather than **grammatical syntax** that the reader will discover his freedom in relation to the process of reading a book, in relation to language.

In all other art forms there are always three essential elements at play: the creator who fabricates the work of art, the medium through which the work of art is transmitted, and the receiver (listener or viewer) to whom the work of art is transmitted. It seems that in the writing of fic-tion only the first and the third elements are at work: the writer and the reader. Me and you. And the medium—and by medium I do not mean the story or the mental cinema one plays while reading fiction, but the language itself—is forgotten. It becomes absent, or rather it is absented, negated by the process of reading, as if it were transparent, as if it were there only to carry the reader into the realm of illusions. Is it because while reading fiction one does not think of the language as being audi-tory or visual (as in music, painting, and even poetry) that it merely serves as a means of transportation from the author to the reader? From me to you, from what I supposedly meant to what you supposedly understand of my meaning? This obsolete form of reading devaluates the medium of fiction, reduces language to a mere function.

If we are to make of the novel an art form, we must raise the printed word as the medium, and therefore **where** and **how** it is placed on the page makes a difference in what the fiction will be for the reader. In other words, we as fiction writers must render language concrete and visible so that it will be more than just a functional thing that supposedly reflects reality. Thus, not only the writer will create the fiction, but all those involved in the producing and ordering of that fiction; the typist, the editor, the typesetter, the printer, the proofreader, and of course the reader will all partake of the fiction. The real medium will be the printed words as they are presented on the page, as they are perceived, heard, visualized (not abstractly but concretely), as they are read by all those involved in the making of the book.

PROPOSITION TWO—THE SHAPE OF FICTION

If life and fiction are no longer distinguishable one from the other, nor complementary to one another, and if we agree that life is never linear, that in fact life is always discontinuous and chaotic because it is never experienced in a straight line or an orderly fashion, then similarly linear, chronological, and sequential narration is no longer possible.

The pseudorealistic novel sought to give a semblance of order to the chaos of life, and did so by relying on the well-made plot (the story line as it was called) which, as we now realize, has become quite inessential to fiction. The plot having disappeared, it is no longer necessary to have the events of fiction follow a linear, sequential pattern in time and space. Nor is it necessary for the narrative to obey logical transitions, or be controlled by a system of cause and effect.

Therefore, the elements of the surfictional discourse (words, phrases, sequences, scenes, spaces, word-designs, sections, chapters, etc.) must become digressive from one another—digressive from the element that precedes and the element that follows. In fact, these elements will not only wander freely in the book and even be repeated, but in some places they will occur simultaneously. This will offer multiple possibilities of rearrangement in the process of reading.

No longer progressing from left to right, top to bottom, in a straight line, and along the design of an imposed plot, the surfictional discourse will follow the contours of the writing itself as it takes shape (unpredictable shape) within the space of the page. In other words, as it improvises itself, the surfictional discourse will circle around itself, create new and unexpected movements and figures in the unfolding of the narration, repeating itself, projecting itself backward and forward along the curves of the writing—(much here can be learned from the cinema, or experiments in the visual arts).

As a result of the improvisational quality of language in this process, the events related in the narration will also unfold along unexpected and unpredictable lines. The shape and order of the story will not result from an imitation of the artificial shape and order of life, but from the formal circumvolutions of language as it wells up from the unconscious.

No longer acting as a mirror being dragged along the path of reality, Surfiction will now reproduce the effects of the mirror acting upon itself. It will not be a representation of something exterior to it, it will be a self-representation. Surfiction will be self-reflexive. That is to say, rather than being the stable image of daily life, Surfiction will be in a perpetual state of redoubling upon itself in order to disclose its own life—**THE LIFE OF FICTION**. It will be from itself, from its own substance that Surfiction will proliferate—imitating, repeating, echoing, parodying, mocking, re-tracing what it will say. Thus fiction will become the metaphor of its own narrative progress, and will establish and generate itself as it writes itself.

This does not mean, however, that the future novel will only be a *novel of the novel*, but rather it will create a kind of writing, a kind of discourse whose shape will be an interrogation, an endless interrogation of what it is doing while doing it, but also a relentless denunciation of its own fraudulence, of what **IT** really **IS**: an illusion (a fiction), just as life is an illusion (a fiction).

PROPOSITION THREE—THE MATERIAL OF FICTION

If the experiences of a human being (in this case those of the writer) occur only as fiction, gain meaning only as they are recalled or recounted, afterwards, and always in a distorted, glorified, sublimated manner, then these experiences become inventions. And if most fiction is based (more or less) on the experiences of the one who writes (experiences that are not necessarily anterior to, but simultaneous with, the writing process), there cannot be any truth nor any reality exterior to fiction. In other words, if the material of fiction is invention (lies, simulations, affectations, distortions, exaggerations, illusions), then writing fiction will be a process of fabricating or improvising on the spot the material of fiction.

The writer will simply materialize (render concrete) experiences into words. As such there will be no limits to the material of fiction—no limits beyond the writer's power of imagination, and beyond the possibilities of language.

Everything can be said and must be said in any possible way. While pretending to be telling the story of his life, or the life story of some imaginary being, the surfictionist can at the same time tell the story of the story he is in the process of inventing, he can tell the story of the language he is using, he can tell the story of the pencil or the typewriter or whatever instrument or machine he is using to write the story he is making up as he goes along, and he can also tell the story of the anguish or joy, disgust or exhilaration he is feeling while writing his story.

Since writing means filling a space (blackening pages), in those spaces where there is nothing to write, the writer can, at any time, introduce material (quotations, pictures, charts, diagrams, designs, illustrations, doodles, lists, pieces of other discourses, etc.) totally unrelated to the story he is in the process of inventing. Or else he can simply leave those spaces blank, because fiction is as much what is said as what is not said, since what is said is not necessarily true, and since what is said can always be said another way. There is no constriction in the writing of fiction, only arbitrariness and freedom.

As a result, the people of fiction, the fictitious beings will no longer be called characters, well-made characters who carry with them a fixed personality, a stable set of social and psychological attributes (a name, a gender, a condition, a profession, a situation, a civic identity). These surfictional creatures will be as changeable, as volatile, as irrational, as nameless, as *unnamable*, as playful, as unpredictable, as fraudulent and frivolous as the discourse that makes them. This does not mean, however, that they will be mere puppets. On the contrary, their being will be more complex, more genuine, more authentic, more true to life in fact, because (since life and fiction are no longer distinguishable) they will not appear to be what they are: imitations of real people; they will be what they are: word-beings.

What will replace the well-made personage (the hero, the protagonist) of traditional fiction who carried with him the burden of a name, an age, parental ties, a social role, a nationality, a past, and sometimes a physical appearance and even an interior psyche, will be a creation, or better yet a creature that will function outside any predetermined conditions of society, outside any precise moment of history. That creature will be, in a sense, present to its own making, present also to its own unmaking. The surfictional being will not be a man or a woman of a certain moment, it will be the language of humanity. Totally free, arbitrary, and disengaged, uncommitted to the affairs of the outside world to the same extent as the fictitious discourse in which it will exist, this creature will participate in the fiction only as a grammatical being (in some cases devoid of a pronominal referent). Made of linguistic fragments often disassociated from one another, this word-being will be irrepressive, amoral, irrational and irresponsible in the sense that it will be detached from the real world, but entirely committed to the fiction in which it will find itself, aware only of the role it has to play as a fictional element.

Since Surfiction will no longer offer itself as a social or historical document that informs the reader about **real life** and **real people**, but as a work of art that functions on its own terms, the reader will no longer be tempted to identify with the characters. Instead the reader will participate in the creation of the fiction in the same degree as the creator or the narrator or the creature of that fiction. All of them will be part of the fictional discourse, all of them will be responsible for it. The writer (just as fictitious as his creation) will only be the point of junction (the source and the recipient) of all the elements of fiction. The story that he will be writing will also write him, just as it will write the reader who gives meaning to the story as he reads it.

PROPOSITION FOUR—THE MEANING OF FICTION

It is evident from the preceding propositions that the most striking and most radical aspects of Surfiction will be its semblance of disorder and its deliberate incoherency. Since, as stated earlier, no meaning preexists language, but meaning is produced in the process of writing and reading, Surfiction will not attempt to be meaningful, truthful, or realistic, *a priori*; nor will it serve as the vehicle of a ready-made sense. On the contrary, Surfiction will be seemingly devoid of meaning, it will be deliberately illogical, irrational, irrealistic, non sequitur, digressive, and incoherent. And of course, since the surfictional story will not have a beginning, middle, and end, it will not lend itself to a continuous and totalizing form of reading. It will refuse resolution and closure. It will always remain an open discourse—a discourse open to multiple interpretations. Surfiction will not only be the product of imagination, it will also activate imagination. For it will be through the collective efforts of all those who participate in the fiction (author, narrator, fictitious being, reader) that a meaning will be formulated. Surfiction will not create a semblance of order, it will offer itself for order and ordering. Thus the reader will not be able to identify with the people or the situations, nor will he be able to purify or purge himself in relation to the actions of the people in the story. In other words, no longer manipulated by an authorial (and authoritarian) point of view, no longer entrapped into the suspension of credibility, the reader will be the one who extracts, invents, creates an order and a meaning for the creatures and the material of fiction. It is this total and free participation in the fiction that will give the reader the sense of having invented a meaning, and not simply having passively received a neatly prearranged meaning.

As for the writer, he will no longer be considered a seer, a prophet, a theologian, a philosopher, or even a sociologist who predicts, preaches, teaches, or reveals absolute truths. Nor will he be looked upon (admiringly and romantically) as an omnipresent, omniscient, omnipotent creator. He will simply stand on equal footing with the reader in their efforts **to make sense** out of a language common to both of them—their collective efforts **to give sense** to the fiction of life. In other words, as it has been said of poetry, fiction will also BE and no only MEAN.

One should, I suppose, in conclusion to such a presentation, attempt to justify, or at least illustrate with examples, the propositions I just made for the present-future of fiction. But justifications and illustrations are readily available, and to a great extent many contemporary writers have already forged their way into Surfiction, or what has also been called postmodern fiction.

For I must admit, I am not alone in this wild undertaking. Many writers in many parts of the world (each in his or her own personal **mad** and **unique** way) have already successfully created the kind of fiction I have attempted to define here. The names of these writers appear in the pages of this volume. However, I am certain that none of them would pretend to have solved all the problems of contemporary fiction. And I do not pretend myself to have done so, nor to have presented the only possible **way of fiction** for the future. I am sure there are other ways, easier, less radical, and more accessible than the one I am proposing, but like most of my fellow-surfictionists, I think this is the path that must be followed and explored if fiction is to have a chance to survive as a serious genre in our complex postmodern world.

It is as a fiction writer, as a surfictionist that I follow this path myself, but not in order to succeed (commercially or socially or in any other way), but in order to transform "the fiasco of reality into a howling success," as the great Samuel Beckett once put it.

4. CRITIFICTION:
IMAGINATION AS PLAGIARISM
(...an unfinished endless discourse...)

I do not care who it is that has or does influence me as long as it is not myself.

—Pablo Picasso

pre-text

We are surrounded by discourses: historical, social, political, economic, medical, judicial, and of course literary. Discourses about sports, about television, entertainment, about pollution, about the weather, about the political situation in Eastern Europe, about the political or religious crisis in the Middle-East, and so on.

Discourses impregnate us, traverse us, guide us, influence us, determine us, confuse us—willingly or unwillingly. We are made of discourses—**words: spoken and written.**

Therefore, the importance of always questioning, always doubting, always challenging these discourses. But less to know what they say, or what they mean, than to find out how they function, how they are constituted, how they become possible within the complexity of our modern world. Obviously, for our purpose, it is the literary discourse that must be questioned. But the problems remain the same. Where and how to begin this questioning? By asking how a discourse is written (and notice, I say **HOW** and not **WHO** writes a discourse)? That is to say, by asking what are the rules (external and internal) that govern a discourse, what are the fundamental norms that permit the formulation of a discourse? And also by asking how a discourse is read? What is the process by which one apprehends a discourse, what are we looking for in a discourse?

These are some of the questions I would like to raise in the following text entitled **CRITIFICTION: IMAGINATION AS PLAGIARISM [. . . an unfinished endless discourse . . .]**. The term critifiction is used because the discourse that follows is critical as well as fictitious; imagination is used in the sense that it is essential in the formulation of a discourse; plagiarism because the writing of a discourse always implies bringing together pieces of other discourses; an unfinished endless discourse because what is presented here is open at both ends, and as such more could be added endlessly.

For centuries it was assumed that **WRITING** (the French call it **ÉCRITURE**) was but a simple act of transmission of a message—**A SOMETHING-TO-BE-SAID**—that preceded the discourse. The one who wrote merely interpreted, transcribed, translated for the reader a meaning that supposedly existed (like an invisible object) somewhere in the universe. Therefore, through the discourse, through writing, the reader came into contact with that meaning—a hidden, true, absolute, and universal meaning. In other words, it was assumed that there was something **PREEXISTING** writing (and speaking too)—*un signifié*, the French linguist Ferdinand de Saussure called it—and writing merely revealed that *signifié* and made it *signifiant* (meaningful).

Thus the **signified** and the **signifier** were one—united. They stuck to each other, matched one another, and the reader received the signified and the signifier at the same time, while words and things (*LES MOTS ET LES CHOSES*, as Michel Foulcault so brilliantly demonstrated in his study by that title) simply overlapped. However, something happened to this neat little system, and today we realize that writing functions as the signified while reading is the signifier. This suggests that it is the process of reading that gives meaning to a text, and not necessarily the process of writing. Consequently, to write is to **PRODUCE** meaning, and not merely **REPRODUCE** a preexisting meaning.

To write is to **PROGRESS**, and not remain subjected by habit or reflexes to *le bon sens* (in its double meaning) which, in fact, is never a *bon sens*— a good or a correct meaning. For if there were a good, a right, a correct meaning in the world, as we were led to believe for centuries, it was so simply because we submitted blindly and passively to the notion of its preexistence.

Reading then is no longer simply to submit, to obey certain rules of logic and semantic, as if one were absorbing meaning (as one absorbs food); reading means learning to read a text while reading it, and in so doing making it pregnant with meaning; it is reading that renders a text meaningful.

One could say then that if it is the act of reading that gives meaning to a discourse, then the act of writing can only be a PRE-TEXT to the eventual meaning the reader will give to that discourse. The text, the completed text, the final text will not only be what is written on paper, but what is also read into the written text. As such, all modern discourses can be called pre-texts—pre-texts in the sense that they precede their eventual meaning, pre-texts because they are reasons, excuses, justifications, springboards, for the ultimate texts.

For instance one could say that Marcel Proust did not write a novel; *A la Recherche du Temps Perdu* is only a pre-text, a pre-novel in search of the novel that the reader completes and renders meaning-**ful** when he reads it. Marcel Proust wrote a three thousand page pre-text to the novel he wanted to write. This is also true of most contemporary novels, especially postmodern novels which often unmake or denounce their meaningfulness while being written in order to accommodate the meaning potential readers will give to these.

In other words, much of today's literature (and especially what has been called Postmodern Fiction or New Fiction or Surfiction) functions as PRE-TEXTS awaiting to become meaningful texts, and we as readers are locked in those pre-texts until we free ourselves from them by giving them meaning. The discourse that I am in the process of writing here is subtitled [. . . **an unfinished endless discourse** . . .] because it is a pre-text that flagrantly exposes how it is made. It reveals as it is written its own lack, its own deficiency, its own meaninglessness, its own unfinishedness, for only the reader will eventually complete this discourse and render it meaningful. As such this essay is a demonstration of how a discourse is formulated, how it is put together, and how it offers itself to meaning-fulness. It is an experimental pre-text to the eventual critical finished text which, of course, will never be written, and ought not be written, since only the reading process can finalize and totalize this discourse and render it meaningful.

_____

CRITIFICTION: IMAGINATION AS PLA(Y)GIARISM

note number one

For **PLAGIARISM** read also **PLA[Y]GIARISM**, for the process of writing at work here is also playful—it is a demonstration, a game, a performance.

note number two

samuel beckett lautréamont severo sarduy jean ricardou denis diderot robert duncan pablo picasso marcel duchamp raymond federman e.h. gombrich philippe sollers david lodge jacques ehrmann maurice blanchot ronald sukenick gilles deleuze john barth michel foucault michel deguy italo calvino marcel proust roberto gonzales echevarria freud jean giraudoux lacan moinous louis-ferdinand céline samuel beckett lautréamont severo sarduy jean ricardou denis diderot robert duncan pablo picasso marcel duchamp raymond federman etceteratceteraetceteraetcete

_____

Somewhere at the beginning of *Les Chants de Maldoror: I shall establish in a few lines how Maldoror was good during the first years of his life when he lived happily. It's done!*

It's done! And the text follows.

The text which I am going to write, and which I am already in the process of writing, is not an attempt to formulate a coherent statement about imagination (thinking!) in literature, or more specifically about the creative process in literature. It is rather a **montage/collage** of thoughts, reflections, meditations, quotations, pieces of my own (previous) discourses (critical, poetic, fictional—*published and unpublished*) as well as pieces of discourses by others (spoken or written—*published and unpublished, authorized and non-authorized*).

These pieces of discourses have been displaced and gathered here for the past few months, not, however, for the purpose of explaining how imagination functions in literature, but rather to illustrate (expose!) how imagination imagines itself imagining; how, to be more precise, imagination does not invent the **SOMETHING-NEW** we too often attribute to it, but instead how (consciously or unconsciously) it merely imitates, copies, repeats, echoes, proliferates—**plagiarizes in other words**—what has always been there.

Indeed, as it was once said: *plagiarism is the basis for all works of art, except, of course, the first one, which is unknown.* Plagiarism, as we all know, and as defined by the most basic dictionary, is the act of copying or imitating the language, ideas, and thoughts of another (thinker, artist, author) and passing off the same as one's original work. And there is no doubt that we listen to others only for the pleasure of repeating what they have said. Yet, we write under the illusion that we are not repeating what has already been written.

The text which I am in the process of writing does indeed fall into the category of pure pla[y]giarism (with a Y because I am also playing here), for I do not know any more where my own thoughts originated, and where these thoughts began to merge with those of others, where my own language began and where it converged with that of others within the dialogue all of us entertain within ourselves, and with others. Therefore, I shall not reveal my sources because they are now lost in this discourse, and because there are no sacred sources for thinking and writing.

But first a poetic statement—an unfinished unpublished and endless poem entitled LISTENING which represent here

diversion number one

JOSEPH LISTENS TO MARY WHO LISTENS TO JESUS WHO LISTENS TO JOHN WHO LISTENS TO SARAH WHO LISTENS TO EZEKIEL WHO LISTENS TO ESTHER WHO LISTENS TO EZRA WHO LISTENS TO JOB WHO LISTENS TO JUDITH WHO LISTENS TO SAMUEL WHO LISTENS TO ESTHER WHO LISTENS TO JOSHUA WHO LISTENS TO JANE WHO LISTENS TO TARZAN WHO LISTENS TO ABIGAIL WHO LISTENS TO JOSEPH WHO LISTENS TO MARY WHO LISTENS TO JESUS WHO . . .

quotation number one

There is no communication because there are no vehicles of communication. Even on the rare occasions when actions and words happen to be valid expressions of personality, they lose their significance on their passage through the cataract of the personality that is opposed to them. Either we act and write for ourselves, in which case action and writing are distorted and emptied of their meaning by an intelligence that is not ours, or else we act and write for others, in which case we act and write a lie.

---

digression number one

Writing, the exigency of writing does not struggle **against** presence in favor of absence, nor **for** it while pretending to preserve it or communicate it. Writing is not accomplished in the present, nor does it present something, nor does it present itself, and even less does it represent, except to play with repetition. *All that is written is fictitious!*

---

quotation number two

Reality, whether approached imaginatively or empirically, remains a surface—hermetic. Imagination, applied [a priori] to what is absent, is exercised in a vacuum, and cannot tolerate the limits of the real. Nor is any direct and purely experimental contact possible between subject and object, because they are automatically separated by the subject's conciousness of perception, and the object loses its purity and becomes a mere intellectual motive or pretext.

---

quotation number three

Oh free us of the never ending utterance!

Therefore, let us cogitate a moment. Writing is not a passive recording of objective reality, but an act of selection based upon an expectancy.

The scientist, the artist, or the writer imposes upon his visual field a concept or model—a **schema**—and then tests, corrects, develops that **schema** with the help of further observations.

Writing is an action. To impose a form of expectancy upon experience is to reduce it to one rather than another kind of order, to modify it, to disturb it, to subject it to control. The choice of a **schema**, along with one's attitude toward it, may be defined as a **stance**, or a readiness for action. Hence, when we attend to the perceptual **stance**, we encounter a set of values that are at once aesthetic, epistemological, moral, and political. And to delineate these values is a signal challenge that tells us when the **stance** is objective.

Classical physics, perspective painting, proscenium theater, and the traditional realistic novel came into being from the same historical impulse. In each, the observer is detached from his subject, stands on a fixed vantage, imposes a **frame** upon the clutter and continuity of experience, and translates a dynamic field into a system that is essentially static and geometrical—a circle at the center of which stands the observer. Paradoxically, the observer (the artist) appropriates his subject while establishing a palpable distance from it. Realism, deriving of course from the Latin *RES*, or thing, aptly applies to this kind of objectification.

---

diversion number two—(an already published poem)

EXCLAMATION MARK

imagine for a moment
that I am
the last man
on EARTH
picture me then
standing
on the edge of the abyss
of HISTORY
like an exclamation mark
at the end of the final sentence
of human speech

---

insertion number one

The world (and by world is meant here the world as it was perceived from the sixteenth century on to the end of the nineteenth century or thereabout) is covered with signs that must be deciphered, and these signs, which reveal resemblance and affinities, are themselves but forms of similitude. To know therefore was a mere interpretation—a process of making objects coincide with words. It meant that one understood the world by going from the visible mark to what was said through it, which would otherwise have remained mute speech, asleep within things.

Quite to the contrary, in our modern age, science, art, and literature are what compensate and not what confirm the meaningful functioning of signs and language. Quantum physics, Postimpressionist art, recent experiments in drama and cinema, and the fiction that follows James Joyce and leads to Beckett and to the Surfictionists deny the possibility of a detached fixed vantage, remove the pregant point from the center of the circle. The subject is no longer enclosed within the frame of the observer's vision. Instead there is a field of energy—usually a self-reflexive field—whereby observer, subject, frame, and medium merge and interact.

In fiction this is expressed succintly by Beckett's **Unnamable** when he wonders about his own ambivalent fictitious predicament and asks: *How can I tell the teller from the told?* And it is true that teller and told, form and content, discourse and story are no longer distinguishable from one another in Surfiction.

---

conclusion number one

Rather than serving as a mirror or redoubling on itself, [sur]fiction adds itself to the world, creating a meaningful reality that did not previously exist. As such fiction is artifice but not artificial. It seems as pointless to call the creative powers of the mind fraudulent as it would to call the procreative powers of the body such. What we bring into the world is per se beyond language, and at that point language is of course left behind. But it is the function of creative language to be left behind, to leave itself behind, in just that way. The word is unnecessary once it is spoken, but it has to be spoken. Meaning does not preexist creation, and afterward it may be superfluous.

---

theory number one

This brings us to the heart of the matter. There are two **myths** that have been perpetuated for a long time about art, about most works of art, and more specifically (for our purpose) about works of literature.

The first is the idea of a sacred source of the work, a sovereign consciousness which is the originator of the work, that is to say, the one who observes, arranges, frames, produces, creates the work of art, and to whom that work of art belongs—the **creator**, the **author**!

Traditionally, the most important, most essential, and most admired attribute of this creator was his imagination—his power to imagine, invent, create something new, something which, supposedly, was not present before. But this is in flagrant contradiction with the notion that meaning precedes or preexists production. For how can an artist (a writer in particular) invent something original if the meaning of what he creates (of what he writes) is already present in the world before he begins his work?

The second myth (closely related to the first) is the idea of originality. The notion that a work of art is good, is great, is true, is beautiful, is valuable, functional even, because it offers itself as original.

Well, I propose that both these myths—that of the sacred source, and that of originality—have reached their end, at last, in much of recent art and literature. In our culture there is no longer any possibility of originality because the day art in general (and literature in particular) began to reflect upon itself, turned inward so to speak, in order to question, examine, challenge, even mock itself, and at times negated or cancelled its purpose, its intentionality, its own means of production and of communication, it abolished these two myths.

By cutting itself from the authority of its creator and his precious imagination, art evacuated from itself (from its center) the imposture of originality. In other words, it stepped out of its own frame—the frame imposed on a work of art by the idea of an origin and a destination. As a result, contemporary (postmodern!) culture could no longer produce original works of art (**masterpieces**), nor could it have great artists (**masters**). It could only produce works of art that resemble one another, and artists who imitate or plagiarize each other's work.

By reflecting upon his work within the work itself, by introspecting the very mechanism of art, the writer discovered (with a certain anguish at times, but also with a sense of self-derision) that he was no longer a supreme, a sovereign, a superior, omnipotent being—a prophet-like figure—in full control of his creation. In fact, he even discovered that he was no longer the sole proprietor of his work since that work was but an imitation, a borrowing, a gathering of pieces of other texts, a plagiarization of other works.

It is in literature especially that the writer confronted the ultimate fraudulence of this romantic notion. For Romanticism supposes (and this concept was handed down to our age through a series of persistent prejudices) that there is a single, omnipotent **creator-proprietor** of the text, and that the text is an expressive entity that stems from a center (**the author**) which is then transmitted to another center (**the reader**). This discovery, in our time, led to the realization that there are no individual proprietors of language, but that in fact language belongs to everyone in the same measure, that language is democratic, and therefore **plagiarism** is the stuff of literature. Or as it was once proposed quite seriously: *plagiarism is not only admissible in literature, it is advisable.*

To write then becomes a surplus, an excess of what has already been written, or what already exists as writing. Thus in contemporary literature all considerations of model, influence, causality, and of course originality, are rendered vain. This means that the act of **plagiarism** cannot come after a text given as initial or original, even if such a text were to exist, for it would itself have been priorly reproduced or imitated or plagiarized. There are no original texts because the first original text has been lost, misplaced, forgotten.

In the light of this realization, the self-reflexive work of literature began to expose the writer as a mere **plagiarist**. Faced with this undeniable evidence, literature (for the past four decades or so) suppressed, eliminated from itself the idea of a central and authoritarian dispatcher of the text and of its meaning.

As already pointed out, **pre-plagiaristic** literature (that is to say the literature that believed in the idea of originality) functioned as though a **something-to-be-said** preceded the text, and the author was the only one who could dispatch that **something** toward the reader, and in so doing the author appropriated that **something-to-be-said** and made it pass for original. Contemporary literature removes itself from that pre-existing secret point of departure known as the origin, which produces the lie of originality. In so doing, it negates the role of the writer as the sole dispatcher of meaning. Furthermore, by reflecting upon itself, by revealing its innermost secrets (its meachnism, it imperfections, its deficiencies, but also its possibilities), contemporary literature drops its mask and exposes its own fraudulence. It reveals that there is nothing sacred or original about the literary creation, and that the writer's imagination is not unlimited and endless, but that, in fact, the writer (even when using his imagination) is merely imitating, parodying, mimicking, repeating, replaying, plagiarizing in other words, not the absolute meaning that supposedly precedes the creative act, but the very medium that constitutes the work of art.

Therefore, today one must accept the fact that literature merely plagiarizes itself, mumbles to itself, draws attention only to its own medium, its language, just as modern abstract painting no longer represents what is exterior to it (reality: Nature and Man), but rather decomposes its own medium, its own material.

The traditional role of the critic (art critic as well as literary critic and historian—the middleman) was to perpetuate these false notions, to veil the truth about the deceptive function of the creator, and the originality of the work of art. The conservative literary critic preserved and glorified the **sacroscanct name** of the author by proclaiming the originality of his work rather than admitting that writing consists of a simple displacement of words. The conservative literary critic performed his function by a process of substitution—he substituted the **name** of the author for the **text**.

In this sense, that critic functioned very much like a traditional Freudian psychiatrist who reduces the neurosis of his patient to archetypes (the father, the mother, the phallus, and the Oedipus complex), who reduces, in other words, adult existence to a mimicry of childhood fantasies.

But in fact, there is no **proper name** in literature, and there is no **original enunciation**. It is the work that ultimately allows the writer to put forth his name. It is not because my name is Federman (the penman, *l'homme de plume*) that I am a writer, but because my books give me the privilege of calling myself a writer whose name happens to be Federman. I cannot substitute my name for my work, nor can my work be substituted for my name. This means that I have no real **authority** over my work, and my work is not necessarily original. This is true of much of contemporary literature. Authors can no longer claim originality for their work, and consequently can no longer pretend to be superior to their readers.

Psychoanalysis uses oedipal reduction and substitution to have the patient believe that he is going to speak in his own name, but it is a trap. He will never speak his own personal words, he will never be allowed to speak his own original words. He will only repeat the words put in his mouth. Therefore, he may speak of wolves, cry like a wolf, act life a wolf, but the psychiatrist thinks dogs, and answers **DADDY**, and the patient repeats **DADDY**, and believes he has gotten rid of the wolf in him. As long as this imposture works it is called a neurosis, but if the patient cracks, if he refuses to say the words put in his mouth, then it is called a psychosis. At the very moment when the patient is convinced that he is speaking in his own name, the conditions of the enunciation are removed.

Traditional criticism performs the same kind of reduction on works of literature, bringing these back to the **proper name** of the author and **the proper psychic (or aethetic) conditions**, thus making it possible to explain and sublimate the mystery of imagination and the lure of originality. But as we have now come to realize, there is no original voice, only a voice within a voice mumbling to itself, only imagination imagining that it is imagining.

----

quotation number four

No trace anywhere of life, you say, pah, no difficulty there, imagination not dead yet, yes, dead, good, imagination dead imagine.

----

insertion number two

The voice at the center of the circle can no longer express what lies outside of it. It can only repeat its own void, its own emptiness, its own absence of fullness. *It can only speak what speaks in it.* That voice can no longer rely on a referential source outside of itself, it can only be a point of departure for the self-proliferation of its speech**LESSNESS**. It can only speak of the **nothing there**—the **nothing new**.

---

quotation number five

The sun shone, having no alternative, on the nothing new.

---

theory number two

This admission of a non-presence (of a gap, a hole) at the center of the work of art is the confirmation that the creator and his imagination have been expelled from it. Of course, conservative antagonistic critics are quick to point out that this situation will bring **THE DEATH OF LITER-ATURE**, but one must reply that literature will not die as long as it continues to question itself, and as long as **WE** (writers, critics, readers) continue to question it, however not to find out who creates the book and out of what obscure source it comes, but to save it from obsolescence.

This means that writers must start all over again and ask, candidly and without prejudice: What does it mean to compose a text? Who composes a text? How is a text composed? Or, to formulate the question in yet another manner: of **what** and by **whom** is a text composed?

These are just so many questions wherein both author and text are reciprocally implicated and are functioning simultaneously and alternatively as subject and object of the questions. The author and the text are therefore caught in a movement in which they do not remain distinct, but rather are transposed and become interchangeable, creating and canceling one another.

Until recently, with regard to literary theory, it was customary to think in one direction only: going from the author to the work, from the subject who creates to the object created. This (linguistic) object was thus recognizable as a **literary object** to the extent that we were aware of having to do with a *gratuitous fabrication of language*. Moreover, that literary object was doubly differentiated from ordinary language: on the one hand, because of its functional character as a work of art—language as instrument of pleasure or of knowledge; on the other hand, because of the fact that ordinary language is not **produced** or **created** by anyone in particular, as opposed to the literary object which is fabricated or constructed by the one designated as "author."

But what if the **author** is no longer to be found at the origin of the **text**? Then to whom does this text belong? These are questions to which the theory of intentionality can no longer provide satisfactory answers. Is the problem of the utilization of a text (its purpose) the same as that of its source (its origin)? Both aspects relate to the question of ownership—that is to say, to the one to whom the text belongs and to the manner in which it is used.

In the light of these questions, one can conclude that every language awaits its author—you, I, anyone—who will make fiction surge forth from it. And one can no longer say that the writer is at the **origin** of his language, since it is language that creates the author and not the reverse. Nor can one say henceforth that literature depends upon the **intention** of the writer on the pretext that he gives the label "novel" or "story" or "poem" to what he writes and that those who partake of the same history and the same culture agree to recognize it as such.

Fiction (or poetry) is therefore not to be found **within** texts of a given (conventional) type, but virtual and diffuse within language itself, that is, in the relationship between writer and writing, reading and reader, and even more generally, in the play of all communication.

---

digression number three

How can a language be recognized as literary?

— By the suspension of the desire for economic advantages.
— By the acceptance of nonsense in language.
— By the perturbation of the logic of ratiocination.
— By indifference toward the efficiency of language.
— By accepting the risk language takes when it speaks.
— By the refusal of influence upon the real through formulas.
— By the retempering of language in the chaos of difference.
— By recognizing the impetuousness of language.
— By admitting the capacity of language for dissoluteness.

---

theory number two *(continued)*

. . . As a result the criterion of originality of artistic production is both modified and contested. **TO WRITE** would be first of all **TO QUOTE**. The writer would not be the one who *listens to a voice from within*, but rather the one who quotes, who puts language into quotes; who both sets it off and calls it to himself, who, in a word, **designates** it as language.

The writer is therefore neither **inside** nor **outside** his language. He does not pause within it. He merely passes through it. But how can we say it is **his** language since the language he places within quotes is a borrowed one? Being a writer no longer corresponds to any particular identity, but to a particular situation, accessible to everyone. This demystification of the sacred position and function of the **AUTHOR** and of the notion of **ORIGINALITY** suggests that, in fact, all writers can be considered **PLAGIARISTS** since they do not invent language but simply quote it from someone else who himself quoted it from someone else, and so on.

To create a literary text is a mere process of displacing, of transposing a set of words from one place to another. In other words, writing—creating, imagining, inventing—is but a simple act of quoting, of repeating the same old thing others have already repeated before. As such, imagination is only the tool that permits such flagrant displacement. This is how literature is made—but also all the other arts, especially the plastic arts—by a process of displacement.

---

insertion number three

One of the great displacers—PLA[Y]GIARIZERS—of the twentieth century, in the field of the plastic arts, was, of course, Marcel Duchamp, who did much to demystify both the idea of the creator and of originality. The core of Duchamp's aesthetic was the dialogue he entertained between himself (projected through his work) and the viewer. He did not believe in an absolute equality between work and public, but in the final triumph of the public, which makes works of art into totems and idols. Nothing made Duchamp scoff more than the notion that an artist's intention governs how his work is received. Thus Duchamp always kept uncertainties, hesitancies, and even unfinished parts of whatever he did, inviting the viewer to finish his art. Duchamp was not afraid to tell us, in his so-called fabrications or found-objects, that he had not invented something original, but that we were all involved in the creative process: that of putting together in a new space things that had always been there before, in order to create a new perception of these things.

Much of contemporary fiction functions in a similar way. It wants its reader to participate, to finish the work; it wants its reader to partake in the sublime absurdity of the creative process. The self-reflexive work of literature allows this relationship, this interplay between the two centers that determine a work of art—the **emitter** and the **receiver**.

---

conclusion number two

One could say then that language is always an excess of language. That in fact, it is only *a rumor transmissible* ad infinitum *in any direction*.

But to play the same old game by the same old rules, to say the same old thing the same old way would merely be competence. Therefore, in order to survive, in order to continue to be, literature must invent new rules for itself—more restraining and constraining rules—even though it is aware that it can only repeat the same old **NOTHING NEW**.

IMAGINATION AS PLAGIARISM—is it an exclamation? Is it a question? A declaration? Or is it simply a statement of facts? Imagination may be plagiarizing itself for lack of anything original to imagine or invent, but that does not mean it is dead. Far from it!

Watch me now, says the old voice of literature:

> *No trace anywhere of life, you say, pah, no difficulty there, imagination not dead yet, yes, dead, good, imagination dead imagine.*

Pah, no difficulty there! And the old displacer of language continues to play and playgiarize.

No, imagination is not dead. What is dead rather is the old notion that in order to be, literature must have a creator and must be original. Contemporary avant-garde literature, in its self-reflexive plagiaristic mode, is working its way toward non-representation and non-expression in an effort to rid itself of the authority of its creator and of the burden of originality. It does so by rendering language seemingly meaningless, expressionless, blank as it were, but also by shifting the property of creation from the author to the reader.

As such imagination imagines how it can still go on while admitting to itself that it can only go on my repeating, by playfully plagiarizing itself—by merely rattling its own rumors and ejaculations.

Or better yet, as **The Unnamable** puts it—that faceless, nameless figure through which language speaks, that grandiose figure which has expelled from its fiction the author and his pretension of originality:

> *I cannot be silent. About myself I need know nothing. Here all is clear. No, all is not clear. But the discourse must go on. So one invents obscurities. Rhetoric.*

5. WHAT ARE EXPERIMENTAL NOVELS AND WHY ARE THERE SO MANY LEFT UNREAD?

The author cannot choose to write what will not be read. And yet, it is the very rhythm of what is read and what is not read that creates the pleasure of the great narratives.

—Roland Barthes

I am playing—playing here on the title of Gertrude Stein's famous essay: "What Are Masterpieces and Why Are There So Few of Them?"

Once upon a time (not so long ago), when the novel was still respectable and respected, when there was even a place in the publishing market-place for the so-called "experimental novel" (or what some people nowadays prefer to call out of timidity "innovative fiction"), one was ashamed to admit not having read all the latest novels.

It was indeed shameful to answer, *No I have not,* when asked, *Have you read Marjorie Morningstar by Herman Wouk?* Or let's say, since we are talking about serious intelligent fiction, *Have you read Lie Down in Darkness by William Styron?* Yes, it was shameful to admit, I have not! Some-how, in those days, one felt guilty for not having read books—all the books, the good books (experimental or not). But then, why should a book make the reader feel guilty? Hell with it!

Then came a time when one would reply, unabashedly, *No I have not read these books yet, but I have read the reviews!* This was the time when, in order to become literature, novels had to be ratified by the proper authorities—such as *The New York Time Book Review* or *The New York Review of Books*.

Today, shamelessly, defiantly even, non-readers answer when asked, *Have you read John Barth's Letters—the entire 722 pages? Oh I read about 30 or 40 pages of it . . . I could only go 1/3 . . . I managed to plow through some 100 pages and then gave up . . . To tell you the truth, that book is unreadable.*

[There are, of course, exceptions—fanatics. Masochistic readers like me, or those whom Gore Vidal calls in an essay openly antagonistic to experimental fiction: "*Gallant readers who risked their all in dubious battle with serious texts, and failed—their names known only to whatever god makes university syllabus, and who have,*" Gore Vidal goes on to explain, "*the courage to read a book that could not, very simply, be read at all by anyone, ever*"].

And the same is usually said of novels like *Ada* (589 pages) by Vladimir Nabokov, *JR* (726 pages) by William Gaddis, *Gravity's Rainbow* (760 pages) by Thomas Pynchon, *Mulligan Stew* (445 large pages) by Gilbert Sorrentino, *Take It or Leave It* (some 500 to 600 unnumbered pages) by the author of this essay. It is true, however, that these are BIG BOOKS (though I fail to see how the size, the length, and even the weight of a book can affect its readability). But what about the novels or stories of Walter Abish, Steve Katz, Ronald Sukenick, Clarence Major, Madeline Gins, George Chambers, and many others who do not write BIG BOOKS, and yet are declared unreadable?

The question then: Is a novel labeled UNREADABLE because it is experimental (*a priori* or *a posteriori*)? Or is it labeled EXPERIMENTAL because it is left unread?

EXPERIMENTAL—it says! Therefore an easy excuse to walk away from the book, to walk out on a novel, and thus fail to assume the consequences of one's relation with the text. How irresponsible: to render invalid the writer/text/reader contract (especially if you have payed your $18.95 or more for the damn book).

Perhaps the time has come again to ask, **What is an experiment? What do we mean by experimental?** Yes, perhaps it is time to go back to the source and check the exact definition of the term, and thus avoid any further confusion.

In my unabridged *Webster's Third New International Dictionary*, page 800, I find this:

> **EXPERIMENT:** *n.* **1 a:** a test or trial (make another ~ of his suspicion—Shakespeare.) **b** [1]: a tentative procedure or policy; *esp*: one adopted in uncertainty as to whether it will answer the desired purpose or bring about the desired result (he is going to put his hope to the test by trying an ~ of bold proportions—Harold Callender) [2]: the tangible result of such a procedure or policy (Benavente's earliest literary ~s were four little romantic fantasies published in 1892—*Current Biog.*) **c:** an act or operation carried out under conditions determined by the experimenter (as in a laboratory) in order to discover some unknown principle or effect or to test, establish, or illustrate some suggested or known truth (the ~s of the defendant's experts lead . . . to the opinion that a typhoid bacillus could not survive the journey—O. W. Holmes, *circa* 1935) **2** *obs*: experience (by sad ~ I know how little weight my words with thee can find—John Milton) **3** *obs*: **expedient, remedy** (you will find it a sure ~ for the quinsy—William Coles) **4**: the process or practice of trying or testing: experimentation (the result of some centuries of ~ tended to raise rather than silence doubt—Henry Adams).

How interesting! How fascinating! Amazing how these definitions always speak to the point (and not without some appropriate irony)— and speak for themselves.

I reflect, my thoughts spinning, skipping, HOPSCOTCHING, (as always playgiaristically):

The usual novel misses its mark because it limits the reader to its own ambit; the better defined it is, the better the novelist is thought to be. We should attempt on the other hand a text that would not clutch the reader but which would oblige him to become an accomplice as it whispers to him underneath the conventional exposition other more esoteric directions. A narrative that will not be a pretext for the transmission of a message—(there is no message, only messengers, and that is the message, just as love is the one who loves).

———————

Lunch with some colleagues from the English Department (one cannot spend all day thinking, writing, messing around with dictionaries). It is the beginning of a new semester; we are talking shop:

— What are you teaching this semester? I ask V. D. to make conversation.
— A graduate seminar on the Contemporary American Novel, V. D. replies.
 I am interested. I go on:—What will your students be reading?
— Oh some Bellow, Malamud, Singer, Roth, Heller, Gardner, and the new Styron. You know, the usual. [V. D. wrote an excellent critical study of the contemporary American Jewish novel].
— If it were not for the last two writers, I say without being facetious, this could be a seminar on the Jewish Novel.
— . . . No John Barth? I ask hesitantly.
— Yes, in fact, an early one. *The End of the Road.* I want my students to be exposed somewhat to experimental fiction, but without boring them with it.
 A piece of bread gets caught in my throat as I ask:—What about Pynchon's *Gravity's Rainbow*? I think, it's an important book in contemporary fiction.
 [I like V. D., he's a serious scholar, and a good buddy—we play tennis together, once a week].— . . . and what about John Hawkes, William Gass, Robert Coover . . . I hesitate . . . Steve Katz, Ronald Sukenick? They are also important contemporary writers.
— Oh, their stuff is unreadable! V. D. says with a grimace on his face.

Unreadable! [He must be annoyed with me, I beat him 6-2, 6-1 last week]. I reflect while chewing on my hamburger deluxe: *How does an English professor determine what is readable and what is unreadable?* I do not say that, I merely think that, to myself.

— And what about you? What are you teaching? I ask C. B. who has been quietly listening to our conversation while eating a club sandwich.
— An undergraduate course on the Modern European Novel.

— I am fascinated. I visualize the poor sophomores struggling with novels by Alain Robbe-Grillet, Philippe Sollers, Maurice Roche, George Perec, Ludovic Janvier . . . [The beast in me thinks French these days, and besides I often regress into the safety of my native tongue whenever speaking of contemporary experimental fiction].

— We're going to start with Joyce's *A Portrait*, C. B. volunteers while taking a bite of his club sandwich, then Kafka's *Metamorphosis*, one Camus, I am not sure which one yet, but probably *The Stranger*, it's the most accessible, then one or two German novels [C. B. has a Ph.D. in Comparative Literature, Anglo/German], Günter Grass, maybe Heinrich Böll, and then we'll finish with one Beckett, an early one, *Murphy*, I suppose, the later Beckett novels are too obscure, too tedious for undergraduates. That's about it, six or seven novels.

— Not a bad reading list . . . no Italo Calvino though? You know, *Cosmicomics, T'Zero, Invisible Cities!* I throw these titles in to impress my colleagues.

— Those books are too difficult, too inaccessible. C. B. has finished his club sandwich, but he goes on while sipping his coffee, I'm not sure my undergraduate students would get anything out of reading these novels. And besides they don't have the necessary background.

Ah yes! The question of necessity!

Gertrude Stein on the subject of **masterpieces** [here you may substitute, if you wish, **experimental novels** for the occasion without, however, assuming that all experimental novels are masterpieces—far from it]: "A master-piece [experimental novel] has essentially **not be necessary**, it has to be that is it has **to exist** but it does not have to be necessary it is not in response to necessity as action is because the minute it is necessary it has in it no possibility of going on." [*my emphasis*].

Exactly! Why bother then with **unreadability**? Especially when it isn't necessary, and there is so much "readable stuff" around.

But then one must also ask: what is **readability**? I cannot resist—here we go again, back to my *Webster's*:

> **READABLE**: . . . that can be read with ease . . . legible . . . pleasing, interesting, or offering no great difficulty to the reader . . . clear in details and significance of symbols . . . that can be read throughout.

I see! **Readability**: what is clear, easy, legible, pleasing, interesting; in other words, what reassures us in a text (a novel) of what we already know, what comforts us because we easily and pleasurably recognize the world (at a glance) and ourselves in the world (at another glance) in what we read. **Readability**: what is instantly and clearly recognizable, and thus orients us, within ourselves and outside of ourselves, in the "reality" of the world. **Readability**: what guides us back from the text to the security of the world, and therefore gives us comfort—**the pleasure of easy recognition.**

Of course: *The author cannot choose to write what will not be read, and yet, it is the very rhythm of what is read and what is not read that creates the pleasure of the great narratives: has anyone ever read Proust, Balzac, War and Peace, word for word? (Proust's good fortune: from one reading to the next, we never skip the same passages).*

That, I suppose is what is meant by **The Pleasure of the Text,** or as Roland Barthes put it in that brilliant little book by that title:

> *What I enjoy in a narrative is not directly its content or even its structure, but rather the abrasions I impose upon the fine surface of the text: I read on, I skip, I look up, I dip in again.*

But there is a paradox here (and Roland Barthes knows this):

> *Read slowly, read all of a novel by Zola, and the book will drop from your hands; read fast, in snatches, some modern text [let's say John Barth's Letters], and it becomes opaque, inaccessible to your pleasure: you want something to happen and nothing does, for what happens to the language does not happen to the discourse.*

First conclusion: If **readability** is the pleasure of recognition (easy pleasurable referential recognition), then **unreadability** must be the agony of unrecognition.

Unreadability: what disorients us in a text (especially in an experimental novel) in relation to ourselves (and I do not mean here the bulk, the thickness, the degree of difficulty, the self-reflexiveness, the tediousness of the text—these are weak excuses for not reading a book). **Unreadability**: what prevents us from recognizing that something is happening, but also prevents us from looking up and away from the text to relocate ourselves in the world. **Unreadability**: what locks us into the language of the text.

Imagine then how lost, how confused, how desperate some unprepared readers must feel when reading a text where *nothing happens twice*, as in some of Samuel Beckett's novels or plays, or where the language moves in a nonsensical direction and therefore *means-not*, as in some of Donald Barthelme stories, or where everything *changes like a cloud as it goes*, as in a Ronald Sukenick novel, or where everything *leapfrogs toward cancellation*, as in my own novels [please excuse the narcissistic reference here, but the beast in me often thinks intertextually when writing about experimental fiction].

But then, as I once proclaimed at the beginning of *Take It or Leave It*: *Writing is not the living repetition of life*. And then added: *Reading is always done haphazardly*.

The pleasure that a readable text affords us is that of recognizing our own knowledge in it, our own culture—of recognizing [*righteously*] how cultivated we are, and consequently how coherent, continuous, whole, rational, logical, how secure we are in our culture. The readable novel reassures us of that.

But what about the unreadable novel then? And precisely, Roland Barthes in *The Pleasure of the Text* makes a crucial distinction between these two types of text:

1. *Text of pleasure: the text that contents, fills, grants euphoria; the text that comes from culture and does not break with it, is linked to a comfortable practice of reading.*
[That would be the readable novel].
2. *Text of bliss: the text that imposes a state of loss, the text that discomforts (perhaps to the point of a certain boredom), unsettles the reader's historical, cultural, psychological assumptions, the consistency of his tastes, values, memories, brings to a crisis his relation with language.*
[That would be the unreadable novel—better known in the supermarkets of books as the experimental novel].

And so here we have it! Second conclusion: (a) The usual, traditional, conventional (readable) novel that which is linked to a comfortable practice of reading and preserves, guards, protects culture; (b) The experimental, innovative (unreadable) novel, that which undermines culture and brings to a crisis the reader's relation with language.

But there is more to this. That comfortableness of readability exists because the text sends the reader back to reality, or allows the reader to play his mental cinema of realism beyond language. And so, once again, readability is equated with **reality**—and lately, even with **morality**.

Deny reality, cut off the referential paths to reality, and your novel will be declared unreadable, and to be unreadable these days, is immoral.

Reflect on your language, write language, examine your relation to language within the mirrors of the text, and you are immediately denounced, accused, and found guilty of **experimentation**, and therefore declared unreadable.

The true writer, we are told by the watchdogs of literature, writes about people, real people, things and events, he does not write on writing, he uses words, but does not reflect on them, does make of words the object of his ruminations. The true writer will be anything but an anatomist of language. The dissection of language is the fancy of those who, having nothing to write, write about writing, and thus create useless and immoral *word-structures*. And these watchdogs of culture and morality are quick to point out that such activities *may be dismissed as little more than the obligatory hyperbole of avant-garde self-promotion, the upping of the ante of extremism that seems necessary nowadays in order to be heard above the competitive din.*

Of course, those who say that are usually the forty-pagers—those who have never really read an experimental novel in its entirety, and that merely for the protection of their own moral good health. But nonetheless, they are quick to advise the novelist that if you want to be **read-[able]** you must write what you see, what you know, what you remember, what really exists in the world, for if you write what you do not see, what you do not know, what you do not remember, if you write only language, you will certainly be **unread-[able]**.

Yet, contradictably, those who deplore that *Literature* has turned *Against Itself* because it is only concerned with its language, the *corruption of language*, and not with social, political and historical reality (or what is still known as Humanism), are willing to concede (since they have no other choice when dealing with serious fiction, and I suppose to save face within the great fiasco of realism) that perhaps novelists should at least attempt to describe *the unreality of reality,* if that is where we are now. Oh yes! Anything to preserve the mimetic imposture. But that is like asking an abstract expressionist (a Clyfford Still, for instance, or a Franz Kline) to paint little recognizable objects in his paintings so that one can at least **see something besides paint.**

Now some people might say that this situation is not very encouraging, but one must reply that it is not meant to encourage those who say that—usually out of despair or out of incomprehension.

Or as Gertrude Stein explains:

> *All this sounds awfully complicated, but it is not complicated at all, it is just what happens. Any of you when you write you try to remember what you are about to write and you will see immediately how lifeless the writing becomes that is why expository writing is so dull because it is all remembered, that is why illustration is so dull because you remember what somebody looked like and you make your illustration look like it. The minute your memory functions while you are doing anything it may be very popular but actually it is dull. And that is what a master-piece is not* [here again make same substitution as before], *it may be unwelcome but it is never dull.*

This brings us to reflect further on the novel in our time: Can it be said that by denouncing the fraudulence of a usual realistic novel that tends to totalize existence and misses its pluridimensionality, the experimental work in a way frees us from the illusion of realism?

I rather believe that it encloses us in it, because the goal of fiction remains the same: it is always a question of expressing, or translating something which is already there—even if to be already there, in this new perspective, consists paradoxically of not being there.

In other words, the novel, in a sense, cannot escape realism, for language too is **a** reality. This mortgage weighs upon it since its origin (but particularly so since the nineteenth century); that is to say since the period when, in order to justify itself of the suspicion of frivolity, the novel had to present itself as a means of knowledge.

However, let us not kid ourselves: reality as such has never really interested anyone; it is and has always been a form of disenchantment. What makes reality fascinating at times is the imaginary catastrophe that hides behind it. The writer knows this and exploits it.

Do you really believe that power, economy, war, peace, sex, violence, all the great tricks of reality (and many others too) would have held for a single moment without the fascination that sustains them, and which comes to them from the inverted mirror of realism in which they are reflected—a fascination that comes from the endless reversion, the sensitive and imminent bliss of their catastrophe, and especially today when reality is but a stockpile of dead matter, dead bodies, dead language.

Edgar Allan Poe was so right in his time when he called nineteenth century realism that pitiable stuff invented by merchants for the depiction of decayed cheeses. Indeed, the ugly beast of realism always stands at bay ready to leap in the moment one begins scribbling fiction. And yet, the history of the novel is nothing else but the success of its efforts to **apprehend** and not **represent** reality—its efforts to substitute finer and more selective mirrors for the vulgar mirrors of reality.

In this sense, the novel, by its very reality, is nothing more than a denunciation of the illusion that animates it. All great novels are critical works (that is to say, experimental self-reflexive works) which, under the pretense of telling a story, of bringing characters to life, of interpreting situations, slide under our eyes the mirage of a tangible form.

From its unthinkable beginning to its impossible end, all fictitious **work** forms a block, an autonomous block: nothing can be taken away from it nor can anything be changed in it. That is what makes of the novel a lure. We think we are going to find in it the expression of our unity, whereas in fact it only manifests the desire of it. We believe, as we are relating ourselves (or being related), that we are going to discover the being that we are already, but that being, that someone, exists only inside the work, and not outside. That being is the product of the book, and not its source. And this because the essence of a literary discourse (experimental or not is finally irrelevant)—that is to say a discourse fixed once and for all (whether we like it or not, whether we read it or not)—is to find its own point of reference, its own rules of organization in itself, and not in the real or imaginary experience on which it rests.

Through all the detours that one takes or that one wishes, the subject who writes will never seize himself in the novel: he will only seize the novel which, by definition, excludes him. And that, of course, is also true of the reader.

And so—final conclusion—as Gertrude Stein wrote: *Always it is true that the master-piece* [experimental novel again] *has nothing to do with human nature or with identity, it has to do with the human mind and the entity that is with a thing in itself and not in relation.* [My emphasis]

And that is **why there are so many experimental novels left unread!**

6. A VOICE WITHIN A VOICE

Sometimes I confuse myself with my shadow, and sometimes don't.

—Samuel Beckett

A voice within a voice speaks in me, double-talks in me bilingually, in French and in English, separately or, at times, simultaneously. That voice constantly plays hide-and-seek with its shadow. Now there is nothing unusual about that. Many people nowadays, in many parts of the world, speak two or three or even several languages. Whether or not I speak French and English well, that is another question which is not for me to answer. But the fact remains that I am a bilingual being, a double-headed mumbler, one could say, and as such also a bicultural being. I spent the first twenty years of my life in France, therefore inside the French language and the French culture, and spent (more or less) the last forty years in America, therefore inside the American language and culture. My social and cultural activities reflect this.

But I am also a bilingual writer. That is to say, I write both in French and in English, and that is perhaps less common. Furthermore, I also, at times, translate my own work either from English into French or vice versa. That self-translating activity is certainly not very common in the field of creative writing. In that sense then, I am somewhat of a phenomenon. The French would say: Federman, *c'est un drôle de phénomène!* And indeed, I have often wondered, as a bilingual writer and as a self-translator, whether I am blessed because of this phenomenon or cursed because of it?

The fact that I am, that I became a bilingual writer may be an accident—an accident of history as well as an accident of my own personal experience. In any case, I am often asked if I think in French or in English, if I dream in French or in English. And I usuallly answer (at cocktail parties, on the golf course, at various intellectual gatherings), since one must always answer such questions if only for the sake of answering something and not be bothered any further with an unanswerable question: *I think and I dream both in French and in English, and very often simultaneously.*

That, in fact, is what it means to have **a voice within a voice.** It means that you can never separate your linguistic self from its shadow.

There seems to be a lot of interest these days in this question of bilingualism and multilingualism, related of course to the current concern for multiculturalism. Recently a friend of mine who is writing a book on the subject of "Bilingual Writers"—such as Vladimir Nabokov, Joseph Conrad, Elsa Triolet, Samuel Beckett, myself, and others—asked me in a letter to reflect on my own bilingual condition, and answer some questions.

Though I exist bilingually, in my life as well as in my work as a poet and a fiction writer, I have never really tried to articulate a theory of my bilingualism. It was, therefore, interesting and provoking for me to answer my friend's questions having to do with what she calls [my friend's name is Elizabeth] the location of bilingualism, the space between the two languages, the verticality versus the horizontality of bilingualism, the periodicities of alternation, the horror of self-translation, etc.

This is what I wrote to Elizabeth in my reply:

> I do not normally question or analyze my schizophrenic bilingualism. I just let it be, let it happen in me and outside of me. I have no idea in which side of my brain each language is located. I have a vague feeling that the two languages in me fornicate in the same cell. But since you are probing into my ambivalent (my ambidextrous) psyche, I can tell you that I believe I am lefthanded in French and righthanded in English. I am not kidding. You see, I was born lefthanded (in Paris, some years ago), but when I broke my left wrist at the age of nine or ten (I forget exactly when now), I was forced to become righthanded. You might say that I am a converted lefty, just as I am a converted Frenchman who became an American. However, there are certain things, certain gestures

and motions which I cannot do with my right hand (like brushing my teeth or throwing a ball), and others which I can only do with my right hand (like writing or playing tennis). Could this have something to do with my bilingualism? It is also true that there are certain texts which I can only write in English, and others only in French, even though eventually I feel a need to translate these texts from one language into the other.

What amazes me, but perhaps it should not, is how true I am to the patterns you describe in your essay [Elizabeth had enclosed with her letter a copy of an essay she had just published entitled "Prolegomena to a Study of Bilingual Writers" in which she delineates certain patterns of behavior for bilingual writers, such as periods of rejection of one language in favor of the other, or a need bilingual writers seem to have to return to their native tongue in the later years of their life]. Considering myself just beyond the midcourse of my literary career, I find that I am more comfortable these days writing in English than in French. This does not mean, however, that I have rejected the French language—my native tongue. I have merely placed it (temporarily) in parenthesis. Though it seems that whenever I begin a new book there is a quarrel inside of me between the two languages to decide which I should use.

Knowing that I have written extensively on the work of Samuel Beckett, Elizabeth asked: *How do you compare yourself to Beckett? And should the case of Beckett be examined? He was such a classical and backward case.* In terms of his bilingualism and the act of self-translating, Beckett was a superman, an angel. He came from above. I am a mere mortal. I come from below, from the cave. Yes, of course, Beckett's case should be examined, carefully examined. In my opinion, Beckett was a most unique, a most extraordinary case of a bilingual writer, for he had, at least since 1945 until his death in 1989, sustained his work in French and English to the point that for him **language one** and **language two** became totally interchangeable. Therefore, when reading Beckett it is absolutely irrelevant to ask which text was written first. His twin-texts—whether French/English or English/French—are not to be read as translations or as substitutes for another. They are always complementary to one another. In many ways, I consider my own work, my bilingual work to be somewhat the same. Whether written in English or in French first, the two texts complement and complete one another.

Is there anything familiar to you in what I am saying in my essay? Elizabeth asked. Yes, most of it, especially the problem of periodicities of alternation (I seem to be constantly vascillating between the two languages), and also what you call *the horror of self-translation* (it scares the hell out of me whenever I begin to translate myself, though lately, in spite of the horror, and even the boredom at times, of translating my own work, I also find a constant temptation to do so, as if there were a profound need in me to see everything I write exist immediately in the other language). There are, however, a few things in your essay with which I seem to differ, but then this may have to do with my own idiosyncratic mind.

For instance, I do not seem to feel, as some of the bilingual writers you discuss (Nabokov and Elsa Triolet in particular), that there is a space between the two languages in me that keeps them apart. On the contrary, for me French and English always seem to overlap, to want to merge, to want to come together, to want to embrace one another, to mesh one into the other. Or if you prefer, they want to spoil and corrupt one another. Therefore, I do not feel that one language is vertical in me, and the other horizontal, as you suggest. If anything, they seem to be standing or lying in the same direction—sometimes vertically and other times horizontally, depending on their moods or their desires. Though the French and the English in me occasionally compete with one another in some vague region of my brain, more often they play with one another, especially when I put them on paper. Yes, I think that the two languages in me love each other, and I have, on occasion, caught them having wild intercourse behind my back. However, I cannot tell you which is feminine and which is masculine, perhaps they are androgynous.

To tell you the truth, Elizabeth, there is perversity in my bilingualism!

Usually when I finish a novel (as you know I have written seven or eight now, either in English or in French), I am immediately tempted to write (rewrite, adapt, transform, transact, transcreate—I am not sure what term I should use here, but certainly not translate) the original into the other language. Even though finished, the book feels unfinished if it does not exist in the other language. Often I begin such an alternate version, but quickly abandon it, out of boredom, I suppose, fatigue or disgust, or perhaps because of what you call "the horror of self-translation," the fear of betraying myself and my own work.

It is curious, however, that when I write something shorter than a novel, a short-story and especially a poem, I immediately do a version in the other language. Most of my poems and short-stories exist bilingually. My feeling here is that the original text is not complete until there is an equivalent version in French or in English. Perhaps the same need for completeness, for finishedness into the other language is there too for the novels, but laziness, fear, apprehension, and of course time prevent me from doing the work. I am aware also that translating one's work into another language often reveals the poverty, the semantic but also the metaphorical poverty of certain words in the other language. There is no doubt that the process of self-translating often results in a **loss**, in a betrayal and weakening of the original work. But then, on the other hand, there is always the possibility, the chance of a **gain**. Yes, the possibility that certain words or expressions in the other language may have the advantage of metaphorical richness not present in the first language. So that even though the self-translator always confronts this possibility of loss, he also hopes for a chance of gain. It seems to me that the translation, or rather the self-translation often augments, enriches, and even embellishes the original text—enriches it, not only in terms of meaning only, but in its music, its rhythm, its metaphoric thickness, and even in its syntactical complexity. This is so because the self-translator can take liberties with his own work since it belongs to him.

However, this matter of loss or gain in the process of self-translation raises a crucial question: whether the translation is merely a substitute for the original or if, in fact, it becomes a continuation, an amplification of the work? We always admire the faithfulness of a translation in relation to the original, and quickly deplore and criticize the liberties a translator takes with the original work of a writer. A case in point: the marvelous though greatly unfaithful translations which Richard Howard recently did of Baudelaire's *Les Fleurs du Mal*, which were bitterly criticized.

Yes, we rarely forgive such liberties, and consequently expect the bilingual writer who translates himself to remain faithful to his own texts. On the contrary, one should allow the writer-as-self-translator some freedom, some room for play within his own work, if only for the sake of enriching that work. And of course, I allow myself such playfulness—often simply for the sake of playfulness, but also in an effort to make sense out of my own writing. But there is another more important reason for wanting to translate one's work: since we know that language is what gets us where we want to go but at the same time prevents us from getting there [I am paraphrasing Samuel Beckett here], then by using another language, the other language in us, we may have a better chance of getting where we want to go, a better chance of saying what we wanted to say, or at least we have a second chance of succeeding. That is to say, we have the possibility of correcting the errors of the original text.

The original creative act, as we all know, always proceeds in the DARK—**in the dark, in ignorance, and in error.** Though the act of translating (and especially self-translating) is also a creative act, nevertheless it is performed in the LIGHT (**in the light** of the original text), it is performed in KNOWLEDGE (**in the knowledge** of the existing text), and therefore it is performed **without error**, at least at the start. As such the act of self-translation enlightens the original, but it also reassures, reasserts the knowledge already present in the original text. Sometimes it also corrects the initial errors of that text. As a result, the self-translation is no longer an approximation of the original, nor a duplication, nor a substitute, but truly a continuation of the work—of the working of the text.

Basically that is how I understand my work as a self-translator and as a bilingual writer. Sometimes the translation I do of my own work amplifies the original, sometimes it diminishes it, corrects it, explains it even (no, not to the reader, the potential reader of the text, but to the author, to myself, who knows very well that the language he uses, whether French or English, is always an obstacle that must be overcome again and again).

That is what I think it means to be a bilingual writer, to be a writer/self-translator. It means that one is constantly displaced from one language (and one culture) into the other. And yet, at the same time, it means that one can never step outside of the languages inside of us, whatever these languages may be. The bilingual writer allows his readers (if he has any) to listen to the dialogue which he entertains within himself in two languages, even though in most cases the readers (who are usually not bilingual) only hear half of this internal (one should almost says infernal) dialogue.

I feel a sense of incompleteness with my work when the texts I have written exist only in one language. This need, this anxiety rather, I have to see my work exist in both French and English . . . (and I should insist, in my own voice—I have read translations of some of my work into French or into English, translations of poems, stories, essays, and even one of my novels done by someone else than myself, and these always feel totally alien to me) . . . this need I have to speak and write in two languages, almost simultaneously, also affects my reading process. Often when I read a book, either in French or in English, a book I am particularly enjoying, a book which gives me, as Roland Barthes put it, *Le Plaisir du Texte*, I find myself translating the text mentally into the other language while reading.

What often troubles me when I am working on a novel in English (and this is because in most of my novels so far, the protagonist remains a Frenchman in exile) is the realization that perhaps it would be easier, and certainly more logical, to write the book in French, or at least to let the protagonist speak French whenever he feels like it. But then, the question can be asked: to whom is the book speaking? My fiction always has an implied reader, or rather an implicit, active interlocutor/listener present in the text, and I believe that this "potential reader" (as I call him) is of the English and not the French language. In other words, my books always seem to be speaking to English reading people, and therefore, even though the central character and even the material are of French origin, they demand to be written in English.

I write more, and have always written more in English than in French, even though English is not my first language. Somehow the French language scares me. It seems to dictate to me how I should write and therefore prevents me from challenging its rules of grammar, whereas English, irrational as it may be in its grammar and syntax, gives me the freedom to experiment with grammar and syntax. Though I did not start learning English until I was twenty years old, I feel that my French is somewhat ancient, perhaps even fossilized, that it is no longer up-to-date, that it is a language of another time in my life. That does not mean that I write badly or poorly in French, I don't think so, nor does it mean that I have rejected the French language, but that when I write in French I become conscious, overconscious of using a language which is distant from me. And this, not because there has been periods when I did not use French (I use my French all the time), but simply because French is somewhat foreign and restrictive to me now. To put is differently, I feel like a prisoner in the French language, perhaps because it made me, because it captured me originally, and I feel free in English because it liberated me, because it took me out of the French language and the French culture.

Is there a desire in me to lose, to abandon French? Elizabeth asked. No, I do not think so. You must understand that I do not feel afflicted with bilingualism, I feel enriched by it. At the same time, however, I do not feel that I want to preserve the purity of my native tongue, as so many of my French friends and colleagues, who have been living and working in the U.S. for many years, often do or claim to do. On the contrary, I want to corrupt the French language in me, I want the two languages in me to corrupt one another.

I have often contemplated writing a book—a book which would probably be unreadable to most people—in which the two languages would come together in the same sentences. There are a few such pages in some of my novels, but I would like to do a entire book using both languages simultaneously. Here allow me to give you a short example of what I mean. It's a passage from my novel *Take It or Leave It*. The French protagonist marvels at what he sees when he arrives in New York:

> . . . *because me too like a jerk j'attendis une bonne heure or more after the phone call à la même place and then de cette pénombre in this gray rain de cette foule en route discontinuous morne surgit around 10:00 p.m une brusque avalanche quite unexpected de femmes absolument belles gorgeous stunning out of nowhere quelle découverte quelle Amérique quel ravissement was I lucky to be here je touchais au vif de mon pélerinage and if je n'avais pas souffert en même temps des continuels rappels the loud gurgling in my stomach de mon appétit wow was I hungry je me serais cru suddenly parvenu à l'un de ces moments de surnaturelle and of surrealistic révélation esthétique les beautés that I découvrais just like that incessantes m'eussent avec un peu de confiance and de confort and a bit more self-confidence ravi à ma condition trivialement humaine . . .*

Yes, I have often considered writing a book in which the two languages would merge into one another. On the cover of this book (if such a book were ever to be published), it would say, **TRANSLATED BY THE AUTHOR**, but without specifying from which language.

There is, quite clearly, an element of playfulness at work in my bilingualism. The two languages play with one another, and I am using the term **play** in its fullest sense—not only in the sense of game, but also in the sense of looseness, as in the expression: *there is looseness in the door*. My French and my English play with one another as two children do in a playground, or rather as two lovers (loose lovers) play with one another in order to possess and even abolish one another. Perhaps my French and English play in me in order to abolish my own origin. In the totally bilingual book I would like to write, there would be no original language, not original source, no original text—only two languages that would exist, or rather co-exist outside of their origin, in the space of their own playfulness.

At this point my reply to my friend Elizabeth stopped abruptly, either because I had nothing more to say, nothing else to invent on the subject of my bilingualism, or simply because I had run out of space. Whatever the case, in the process of reflecting about bilingualism, I think I had managed to explain (especially to myself) how the struggle, the love affair, and the playful intercourse of the two langugages in me have determined and informed my work over the years.

No, I do not feel afflicted by my bilingualism. I feel enriched by it, as I hope the following bilingual poem will demonstrate:

OLD SKIN——VIEILLE PEAU

sixty already——soixante ans déjà
and still not a word——et pas encore un mot
mumbling like a fool——balbutiant comme un con
at best——au plus
two or three groans——deux ou trois cris
that's about all——voilà c'est tout
lots of qua qua——beaucoup de qua qua
that's how it is——voilà comment c'est
in the bubble of the skull——dans la bulle du crâne
dragging yourself in verbal mud——te traînant dans la boue verbale
looking for a word——cherchant un mot
the first word——le premier mot
a noun perhaps——un nom peut-être
a verb——un verbe
yes——oui
an imperative——un impératif

7. FEDERMAN ON FEDERMAN: LIE OR DIE

(Fiction as Autobiography/ Autobiography as Fiction)

All that is written is fictive.
—Stéphane Mallarmé

If I were a critic (which I was once upon a time) and were asked to discuss (in spoken or written form) Federman's fiction, I would not discuss what Federman has written in his books (those curious books which seem to defy any classification and yet call themselves novels with effrontery) but what he has left unwritten. I mean unwritten not only in terms of substance and content, but also in terms of form and language. His books are full of holes, full of gaps, full of missing elements, to use an oxymoron. And his language too is full of holes, full of missing parts. His books are, in fact, always left unfinished. Federman writes unfinished stories made of unfinished sentences but which pretend to be finished stories made of finished sentences. Look for instance at the ending of *Take It or Leave It*:

> *and so he folded himself upon himself like an old wrinkled piece of yellow paper there on that hospital bed as I took leave of him (on the edge of the precipice) closed himself like a used torn book that nobody needs any more a useless book to be thrown in the garbage as he thought of the trip the big beautiful journey he could have made cross country coast to coast and which someday he could have told like a beautiful story or retold*

> *with all the exciting details to a friend or to some gathering of interested*
> *listeners with all the passion necessary to tell such a fabulous story*
> *directly or indirectly but now it was finished cancelled cancelled and so*
> *empty of his last drop of courage and the last words of his story which is*
> *now cancelled cancelled since they were shipping him back to where it all*
> *started he said sadly to himself: no need trying to go on no . . . but per-*
> *haps next time yes the next time . . . (so long everybody)*

Federman's latest novel, *To Whom It May Concern,* also ends on a note of unfinishedness when the narrator-writer declares:

> *And so, as I continued to listen to the cousins, their faces fading into*
> *darkness, their voices becoming more and more faint, I realized that their*
> *story would always remain unfinished . . .*

Therefore, when dealing with Federman's work, one must accept the fact that what makes up his fiction is not necessarily what is there (that is to say what is told, what is visible, what is readable, what is present, what is presented, what is represented or appresented) but what is not there (what is not told, what is not visible, not readable, not presented, not represented or appresented). In other words, what is important to notice in Federman's fiction is what is absent.

And indeed, the fundamental aspect, the central theme of his fiction is ABSENCE. Federman writes in order to cancel, or better yet, in order to absent the very story he wants to tell. In the same process, Federman writes to absent (or, to use a contemporary term, to deconstruct) the very language he employs.

As the commentators of his work have often noted, Federman has perfected the art of cancellation and absence, and he has done so with cunning and devious stratagems. Therefore, what the critic should discuss in his work are the holes, the gaps, the voids, the empty spaces, the blank pages, and of course the closets, the precipices, and especially the four X-X-X-X's which are the recurring key terms that point to that absence.

Yes, what must be apprehended in Federman's fiction is what is missing, what has been deliberately or perhaps unconsciously left out. But not because what is missing could not be told or written (such as the unspeakability of the Holocaust that informs Federman's life and work, and which he refers to in one of his novels as **The Unforgivable Enormity**), but because Federman is primarily writing to demonstrate the impossibility and the necessity of the act of writing in the Postmodern/ Post-Holocaust era. As such he seems to suggest that in order to be able to write under today's moral, social, psychological and political conditions, one must lie (one must fill the holes), for if one cannot lie (cannot fill the holes), one will certainly die (as a writer that is).

Let us then approach the subject at hand—AUTOBIOGRAPHY AS FICTION or FICTION AS AUTOBIOGRAPHY in the context of the avant-garde—on the basis of this central idea in Federman's work: that in order to survive (which also means in order to be able to write) one must lie. In this respect, one could say that what is missing from his work (since it is presented as a lie) is the truth—the paradoxical truth that says that in order not to die (as a writer) Federman must lie about his life (as a human being).

LET US BEGIN THEN (TO LIE OR TO DIE)

There seems to be a great deal of interest these days in biography and autobiography—not only on the part of scholars and writers, but on the part of people in general. Why? Is it because people are in need of guiding figures or heroic models to admire or emulate? Or is it simply because people are curious about the private lives of the famous (or the not so famous)? Or is it because people are seriously interested in others, in the lives of others rather than just their own? Or only interested in gossip, in the dirty laundry kept in the private closets (or not so private closets) of those who have gained fame and wealth? Whatever the reason, the question of biography and autobiography is certainly interesting, but also problematic, for one must always approach a biography (a life told by someone other than the one who lived it) and even more so an autobiography (a life told by the one who lived it) with a great deal of suspicion as to the reliability of its facts.

The essential question then: how to replace a life in its context when in most cases one has forgotten or falsified the original text?

Fiction writers are often asked (and I am no exception): "*Is your fiction autobiographical?*" And the writer usually replies, somewhat embarrassed, as if the fact that he used elements of his own life was an embarrassing matter: *"Yes, I suppose one could say that my fiction is autobio-graphical, but I must emphasize that I have distorted facts in order to achieve a distance from myself . . . an aesthetic distance,"* the writer adds, de-emphasizing the last part of his reply as if unsure of its meaning.

I have often wondered if that means that a life in itself cannot be aes-thetic, that a life has to be fictionalized in order to acquire an aesthetic quality?

Whenever a fiction writer apologizes for having written about his own life, or for having assigned to his characters certain aspects of his own experiences, he seems ashamed to admit it, as if ashamed to have lived, to have had interesting, dramatic, perhaps even traumatic experiences, or else ashamed to admit to have had a boring, trivial, uninteresting existence. Some of the great novels of all times were based on boring, trivial, even uninteresting experiences. The fact that a disabused, mid-dle-aged gentleman remembers how he used to drink tea with his grandmother when he came home feeling sick and depressed, and how he used to dip a piece of cake called *une petite madeleine* into his tea, is not a very exciting, not a very profound experience, and yet one of the greatest novels ever written comes out of this banal gesture and this insignificant cup of tea. I mean, of course, Marcel Proust's *A la Recherche du Temps Perdu*.

I believe that a fiction writer should never apologize for writing auto-biographical novels. On the contrary, *"a writer should have the courage of his own narcissism,"* as I once told an interviewer who seemed disturbed when I openly admitted to him (without apologizing) that indeed my fiction is based on experiences of my life—*"real or imagined,"* I empha-sized without trying to be facitious. I suppose this calls for an explana-tion.

There is a statement that runs through all my fiction (spoken either by one of the characters or else by the author himself), a statement also repeated in the various essays I have written about contemporary fic-tion. It goes like this: *"A biography is something one invents afterwards, after the facts. Therefore, in order to be recorded in history, one must either lie or die."*

I originally borrowed this statement from Céline whose fiction is cer-tainly outrageously autobiographical, or rather whose fiction denounces itself as being outrageously autobiographical. However, I distorted that statement somewhat to serve my own purpose. Céline, of course, much as I do in my work, used his own life, his own experiences as a Frenchman, as a survivor of World War I, as a wanderer during World War II, but also his experiences as a writer and as a medical doctor to create his fiction. In my case, I can say that it is as a wandering French Jew who became an American, as a survivor of the Holocaust during World War II, but also as a writer and a professor/critic of literature that I create my fiction.

In other words, as the subtitle of this presentation suggests, fiction and autobiography are always interchangeable, just as life and fiction, fact and fiction, language and fiction, that is to say history and story are interchangeable. And this because, for me, the STORY always comes first. Or to put it slightly differently: everything is fiction because everything always begins with language, everything is language. The great silence within us must be decoded into words in order to be and to mean.

"In the beginning was the word." Thus begins one of the ancient texts that still governs how we relate to the world. In the beginning was the word, that is to say language, and when we say language of course we immediately mean story and story-telling: fiction, fable, myth, theology.

Yes, everything (life, history, experiences, even death) is contained in language. Everything is language, language is everything. Whether we think of language as a blessing or as a curse, we cannot escape it. But we must accept the fact that it is both a means of communication and an obstacle to communication, or as Samuel Beckett once put it: *"Language is what gets us where we want to go and prevents us from getting there."* It is in this sense then that an autobiography, or for that matter a novel, can never reach its destination, never achieve its purpose: tell the complete and truthful story of a life.

An experience, whether tragic, comic, or banal, only gains meaning when it has passed through language, when it has been recounted, recorded, told, spoken, or written. But since language is always deficient and unreliable, the recounting of an experience is also deficient and unreliable. As such, meaning is never absolute and cannot precede an experience, nor can it precede language. Meaning is produced by language. The act of speaking or writing is what produces meaning. It is in this sense that the meaning (or the truth) of an experience, or the meaning (or the truth) of history comes after it has happened, after the facts. History, whether collective or individual, is made of the stories one tells of what happened.

If one accepts this idea [and I must confess that a good many nervous critics who still believe that "*meaning precedes language, or essence precedes existence*" have argued with me about this] then one can say that it is the FICTION of a writer which informs his LIFE, and not necessarily his LIFE which determines his FICTION.

It is only because Balzac or Flaubert or Faulkner or Beckett wrote novels that we can speak of their lives (in a meaningful literary sense). It is their books which designates them as writers. Only after the writer has written his fiction can one ask if it is autobiographical.

Paradoxical as it may seem, only fiction is real, only fiction is true. The rest cannot be verified for it remains in the domain of absence, in the domain of what has already happened in the past, and the past can never be totally recaptured, as writers quickly learn in the process of writing fiction or their autobiography. Again, this needs further clarification [with a personal illustration this time].

LET US CLARIFY THEN (TO LIE OR TO DIE)

A couple of years ago a major publisher approached me to write a mini-autobiography (mini, because from the start the publisher limited me to a ten thousand word text). I told the publisher, half-jokingly, that with such a word limitation, I could only give him the story of the first twelve years of my life, especially since these twelve years had been packed with so many dramatic events. This mini-autobiography was to be included in a series of volumes that contain other such "essays in autobiography," as the publisher called them, written by various contemporary authors.

At first I was reluctant to accept this offer. I felt that it was somewhat premature for me to write the story of my life, and besides my fiction was already the story of my life—or is it the reverse? But I accepted (after all the publisher was offering me a rather handsome fee), and wrote what I eventually called: *A Version of My Life—The Early Years.*

The early years because I chose to deal with moments and events of my life only up to 1971, the year when my first novel, *Double or Nothing*, was published.

My autobiography is not only a written text, but it also contains a dozen or so photographs which illustrate certain moments of my life. The title, of course, immediately throws an element of doubt and duplicity over the text: A VERSION OF MY LIFE. One could ask, which version? And if there are other versions, which is the true version, the real version, the more reliable version? One could also ask, does that mean that the facts related here may not be correct, and therefore may not be trusted?

The photographs in the text do not lie, at least as far as photographs supposedly freeze the subject in time and space. It is really me that one sees there in various places, at various moments, and with various people (my sisters, my wife, my daughter, friends, fellow-writers, my dog). But the text: can it be trusted? Can the language of the text be trusted? And even less so, the events related by that language? There is no way to verify, no way to ascertain the veracity of what I have written. The reader of my autobiography can only **take my word[s]** for it. Indeed, the reader of an autobiography can only believe the words the writer has used, even though he knows that these words are deficient and unreliable.

Because of the unreliability of language, I cannot deny nor affirm that the facts related in my autobiography have or have not been distorted from the truth. Similarly, an artist who paints a self-portrait cannot claim that he has really painted himself since he knows that the medium he uses (paint) only creates an illusion. Autobiographies and self-portraits are always distortions of reality because they are created on the basis of a memory or an image, with words or with paint.

I have often wondered how a painter creates a self-portrait. Does he stand before a mirror, or does he paint himself while looking at another picture (a photograph or a sketch), or does he simply work from memory? But then can the artist trust the image he has of himself—in his mind or in his portfolio? These are very intricate questions which raise a whole problematic of not only self-portraits but autobiographies.

For instance, what was Velasquez looking at when he painted himself in the process of painting the painting that we are looking at: the famous *Las*

Meninas? Even more interesting and problematic is the painting by the Austrian artist, Egon Schiele, entitled *Portrait of the Artist Masturbating*. One can only wonder how and when Schiele observed himself in order to be able to paint himself in the process of doing what he has represented?

These are some of the questions that came to my mind when I began writing my autobiography. These forced me to reflect on what I was doing, on the very idea of an autobiography, that is to say, to reflect on the subject I am addressing here.

An autobiography is never the complete history of the person who writes it. By necessity (of space, of language, of prudishness perhaps, of humbleness even, of time) it must be selective. The autobiographer functions very much like the novelist who obviously selects what he will tell or not tell about his characters. Right from the start I had to make choices about what I would include in the ten thousand words that were prescribed to write the story of my life. Would I write mostly about my family—my ancestors, my parents, my wife, my children? Or would I write mostly about myself? Should I concentrate on my childhood, my education, my travels, my adventures and misadventures, my love life, or even my sexual life? Should I write mostly about what I am today? In other words, would I write from a civil, a familial, a social, a psychological point of view, or would I write strictly from a personal, self-centered point of view? Would I reveal all—my fantasies, my ambitions, my failures, my qualities, and my vices?

Obviously, limited as I was by the number of words assigned to me, I had to limit myself to only certain aspects and certain moments of my life. But then this is also how I write my novels—by a process of selection and cancellation.

I finally decided that I would write about those moments and those events in my life which made of me a writer. That is to say, I would write about those experiences (happy or unhappy, sad or funny as they may have been) which ultimately became my fiction. For this reason, I gave each section of this autobiography a title which happened to be the title of one of my novels. I did this to show clearly the relationship between my fiction and my life—between autobiography and fiction, or vice versa.

What amazed me while writing this autobiography was to what extent I was borrowing from my novels, literally lifting whole passages, paragraphs, sentences. I was plagiarizing myself. My fiction was nourishing the story of my life. It felt as if I were writing not about myself, but about the fictitious life of someone whose name happens to be Raymond Federman. This forced me to reflect further on the notion that a biography is always something one invents after the facts.

In my novel, *The Twofold Vibration* [1982], the protagonist (an unnamed Old Man who is to be deported to the space colonies on New Year's Eve 1999) is asked by one of the narrators to tell the story of his life, and the Old Man replies: "*I have no story, my life is the story.*" But then he changes his mind and says: "*No, the story is my life.*"

THE STORY IS MY LIFE (TO LIE OR TO DIE)

What I finally wrote in my autobiography is not really the story of my life, but the story of how I became a writer because of certain experiences I had during my life. That is why I could only write A VERSION OF MY LIFE—a manipulated version. This is how it begins:

> *I often wonder if being a writer, becoming a writer is a gift one receives at birth, or if it happens accidentally in the course of one's life. I am always envious—and suspicious too—of those who say to me: "I wrote my first poem when I was eight years old, and published my first story when I was fifteen." It makes me feel that perhaps I wasted the first twenty-five years of my life.*

> *Even today, after the millions of words I have scribbled (in English and in French) over the past thirty years, with seven novels in print, one more in progress, one abandoned, three volumes of poems, several books of essays and criticism, hundreds of loose pieces of prose and poetry in magazines, and much more still unpublished, I often doubt that I am a writer. Thirty years of trying to convince myself of this fact. Thirty-four years, to be exact, since my first published poem in a college magazine in 1957—a five line poem entitled "More or Less." It went like this:*

From Cambrian brain-
Less algae sprung the ten-ton
Flesh and bone reptile
Then man from Ape till bodi-
Less brain shall inherit the Earth

A ponderous little poem which certainly does not indicate that I was then or would ever become a writer. Even now I believe I am still working at becoming one, and perhaps I shall die never knowing whether or not I was a real writer. It seems to me that everything I write (and few days pass that I do not sit at my desk to work) is a preparation for the great book that someday will make of me the real writer. Meanwhile my books are published, reviewed, discussed, analyzed, criticized, translated, praised and attacked, a couple even received literary prizes, and still I am not sure.

The other day my best fan, my lovely daughter Simone, on the phone from New York City (collect of course) says to me, of without malice, lovingly in fact: "Hey, Pop, I think I know what your epitaph will be, I mean, you know, what should be written on your tombstone: OUT OF PRINT!" What gentle brutality. She's got it right though, there is brutality in what writers do. Writing is such an inhuman thing to be doing, so brutally asocial, unnatural. So much against nature. No wonder writers suffer fits of doubt and despair.

No, I do not think I was born a writer (even though I too can doubt and despair like a true writer), but the accidents of my life may have helped make of me a writer. If I was given a gift at all which forced me to write, it was what happened to me, often in spite of myself, during the first twenty-five years of my life. Much of the fiction I have written found its source in those early years.

In a recent article about my fiction, the critic Marcel Cornis-Pop states, rightly so I suppose, that "unlike some of his metafictional contemporaries, [Federman] has been blessed (or cursed) with enough biography for several epic cycles, condemned to string out the story of his life endlessly in various fictions." The first twenty-five years of my life certainly contained enough drama, enough adventures, misadventures and misfortunes to inspire several novels. I lived those years oblivious to myself and to the sordid affairs of the world around me, unaware that the experiences I was living, or I should say enduring, would someday make a writer of me. My life began in incoherence and discontinuity, and my work has undoubtedly been marked by this. Perhaps that is why it has been called experimental.

"My life began in incoherence and discontinuity," but I could also have written, "My life began with doubt and uncertainty." Whatever the case, it is true that my work has been marked by this uncertain, incoherent, doubtful, discontinuous beginning, and that in order to be recorded in history, or better yet in order to be able to record my life in a story, I had to lie—to lie so that I could survive, and not die.

"My death is behind me," says the Old Man in *The Twofold Vibration*, who is also a survivor and a novelist.

To lie or to die! That is the writer's dilemma, or rather the writer's paradox. Echoing Zeno's old paradox—THE LIAR'S PARADOX, *"All Cretans are liars, I am a Cretan."*—I can say for all writers and for myself too: *"All writers are liars, I am a writer,"* thus preventing all possibilities of questioning the veracity of my work.

THE LIE OF AUTOBIOGRAPHY/THE TRUTH OF FICTION

A few years ago at a literary conference in San Francisco, where I was presenting a paper and reading from my fiction, a critic, an antagonistic critic questioned, in public, before a large audience, the truth of the most important and most traumatic moment in my life—of my autobiography. He questioned the truth of what I have called **The Closet Experience**, which is well-known to those who are familiar with my books. This is how that experience is related in my autobiography:

> *I was born in Paris, France, in 1928, May 15, a Taurus, which means one who lives in the world with his feet on the ground and his head in the clouds. But if this is my official date of birth, it was not until July 16, 1942, that my life really began. On that day, known in France as* le jour de la Grand Rafle, *more than twelve thousand people (who had been declared stateless by the Vichy government and forced to wear a yellow star on their clothes bearing the inscription* JUIF) *were arrested and sent to the Nazi death camps. That day, my father, mother, and two sisters were also arrested and eventually deported to Auschwitz where they died in the gas chambers. There are records of this. I escaped and survived by being hidden in a closet. I consider that traumatic day of July 16, 1942, to be my real birthdate, for that day I was given an excess of life.*

The critic in question said that I had invented this event, invented this whole closet story, given myself that traumatic experience in order to be able to write, in order to give my fiction a dramatic, and even a sentimental quality. He insisted (he was very stubborn and agressive), in public, before some of my friends who were present at that conference, that I had never been hidden in a closet during World War II, that my parents and sisters were never taken away to a concentration camp to be exterminated, that in fact they were well and still living somewhere in the world. Yes, he insisted that I had invented the whole thing, and who knows, some of the people in the audience may have been convinced by what he said. Listening to him, I myself began to doubt the very experience on which much of my fiction has been built. Could it be that none of that had happened, that I was never hidden in a closet, that in fact during World War II I was safely protected from all the horror, that none of what I wrote in my novels really took place, that I dreamt the whole thing, that I simply made up the whole story to draw attention to myself, to inspire myself? After all, it is a rather good story.

Here is how that story is retold to the author of the book by one of the narrators in *The Twofold Vibration* as told to him by the Old Man:

The soldiers were already in the courtyard, calling their names, his voice sounded remote, it was early in the morning, very early, five in the morning, in July, I think, or perhaps August, hard to remember, and the mother quietly awoke the boy, he was only twelve then, she was crying softly, shh, shh, the boy must be saved, she whispered as she gently pushed him into a closet, he was wearing his little boy shorts, a closet just outside the door of their apartment, on the landing, on the third floor, it was impossible to tell if the Old Man was inventing what he was relating or remembering it, a dark box where they kept old clothes, empty skins and dusty hats, he called them, and old newspapers, and after the soldiers took away his mother, his father, and his two sisters, stumbling down the staircase with their nomad bundles, as he called them, moaning yellow stars on their way to their final solution, to be made, remade to shade the light, is how he put it, and all was quiet, the little boy sat on a pile of newspapers, still half-naked listening to voices behind the walls while sucking pieces of sugar cubes he had found in a box behind the newspapers, eyes burning with colorful circles he sat there for hours, waiting, I suppose, for night to fall so he could come out of his hole . . . later, in the afternoon, hands groping in the dark, dust in his mouth, butterflies in the stomach, guts squeaking with pain, yes the poor boy had to go to the bathroom, and he felt guilty about not being able to do it in the proper place, he unfolded a newspaper and crouching like an animal, like a sphinx, he defecated his fear holding his penis away from his legs not to wet himself, then he wrapped it into a neat package, smelling the warmth on his hands afterwards, and when finally it was dark outside, and the trains were rolling into the night to the East, he climbed the ladder near the door of his closet up to the skylight and placed his filthy package on the roof, the Old Man smiled, for the birds, I suppose, or to disintegrate in the wind and become, years later, the symbol of his strange rebirth . . .

It is true, after all, that there is no way to verify, to prove that what is told here really happened to me. No way to ascertain that what I have been recounting over and over again really occurred. From an early poem published in 1958, entitled "Escape," to my latest novel, *To Whom It May Concern,* I have been circling around that closet experience, digging into that obsession, telling the same old story, and yet there is no way to know if it truly happened to me.

Here is that 1958 poem:

ESCAPE

My life began in a closet
among empty skins and dusty hats
while sucking pieces of stolen sugar

Outside the moon tiptoed across the roof
to denounce the beginning of my excessiveness
backtracked into the fragility of my adventure

Curiosity drove me down the staircase
but I stumbled on the twelfth step and fell
and all the doors opened dumb eyes
to stare impudently at my nakedness

(continued)

As I ran beneath the indifferent sky
clutching a filthy package of fear in my hands
a yellow star fell from above and struck my breast
and all the eyes turned away in shame

Then they grabbed me and locked me in a box
dragged me a hundred times over the earth
in metaphorical disgrace
while they threw stones at each other
and burned all the stars in a giant furnace

Every day they came to touch me
put their fingers in my mouth
and paint me black and blue

But through a crack in the wall
I saw a tree the shape of a leaf
and one morning a bird flew into my head

I loved that bird so much
that while my blue-eyed master
looked at the sun and was blind
I opened the cage and hid my heart
in a yellow feather

No, there is no way to know if I was locked in a closet when I was a little boy, if the moon tiptoed across the roof that night, if I stumbled on the steps while going down the staircase, if the doors opened to stare at my nakedness, if a bird really flew into my head, and so on. And what about the filthy package of excrement left on the roof? Who can believe that? It was dark that night. No one saw the boy. There were no witnesses. And if there were some, by now they must either be lost or dead, or have forgotten the whole sordid affair.

And so, Federman has perhaps been lying about his life, or else he has been inventing for himself an experience so that he could write it. Or even better, Federman has borrowed that experience from someone else, and has attributed it to himself. Writers often do that, borrow stories from others. After all, Federman has openly stated, on several occasions, that all writers are pla[y]giarizers.

It is even possible that in repeating the same "second-hand story" over and over again—the story of the closet, but also the story of the raw potatoes on the train, the story of the farm, the story of the journey to America, of the factory in Detroit, the story of Charlie Parker and the tenor saxophone, and of the Buick Special, and all the other stories he has told—Federman convinced himself of the truth of these fictions.

After all, it is well known that many children were hidden in closets or abandoned in train stations during the Second World War. Therefore, the story of Federman's closet becomes rather common and banal. It could be anybody's story. Everybody's story.

And so, that day in San Francisco, I had no argument, no refutation to offer to that critic who questioned the truth of the experience that nourishes my fiction. No, I had no proofs to convince him of the truth. I only had my fiction—my lies. But then isn't it imagination (or lies—same thing) that fills the holes of absence?

However, something important should be added here, important in relation to the questioning of the facts of my life. After having denounced me publicly, the young critic concluded by saying (and this is crucial to our topic): *"Mister Federman, I may be suspicious of the facts of your life, I may not trust your biography, but I must admit that I am totally convinced by the stories you tell in your novels. Not only convinced, but deeply moved by them. I trust your stories."*

This was a most unexpected reversal, a most amazing way of concluding his argument. For suddenly he was no longer an antagonistic critic, but a sympathetic reader of my fiction. Of course, what is interesting is that he expressed doubt about the truth of my life, and showed trust in a fiction supposedly based on my life. However, by questioning the veracity of certain facts of my life, he raised the crucial question of the equivocal relationship that exists today between facts and fiction, between biography and fiction, between memory and imagination.

This sudden reversal was important to me because I do not think that I became a writer in order to tell the story of my life. I became a writer in order to tell stories. And I am sure this is true of all those who call themselves writers. If some of the stories I have told happened to be based on my life, finally it is totally irrelevant—especially when it comes to judging the quality, or the efficacity, or even the beauty of my fiction.

The real question then about **Autobiography as Fiction** or **Fiction as Autobiography** is this: do we read fiction simply to find out about the life of the author, or because we are interested in people, interested in the human condition? If we are interested only in the life of the author, then why not simply ask the author to tell the story of his life, why not simply read his autobiography. But if he does tell the story of his life, can we trust it? Can we trust him or her? No, I do not believe that we read fiction to learn about the life of the author. If this was the reason for reading novels, or for listening to a writer talk about his work, the entire enterprise of literature would become trivial, boring, derisive, uninteresting.

What is interesting in the relationship between fiction and autobiography is the mechanism by which a writer transforms elements of his life into stories. What is fascinating is the process which makes it possible for a life to become fiction, or vice versa for fiction to make it possible for a writer to have a biography—real or imagined.

AVANT-GARDE AUTOBIOGRAPHY
(TO REMEMBER OR TO IMAGINE)

Until very recently one read novels—especialy those written in the first person—as though they were mere autobiographies, and it was assumed that the writer merely wrote what he **remembered** of his life, of his youth, of his family, of his amorous adventures. Consequently, **memory** (voluntary or involuntary) was considered the sole mechanism that made personal or autobiographical fiction possible.

For a long time then, *A la Recherche du Temps Perdu* was read as just a straight autobiographical novel. The life of Marcel Proust and that of Marcel (the narrator-protagonist of that gigantic novel) were considered to be the same. Of course, this was totally wrong. Certainly Marcel Proust used elements of his life and of the life of his time, but Marcel in the novel does not merely remember what happened to him when he was younger and lived the life of a dilletante, in most cases he invents, he speculates, imagines, makes-up stories about himself and the other characters in the novel. Yes, Marcel constantly invents, right before our eyes, what he thinks happened, or might have happened, or ought to have happened, especially since, in many instances, he was not present himself to witness what happened, or if he was present he was unable to hear or see what was happening. That is, in fact, the key to this novel: that Marcel does not simply remember what he tells us, but that he speculates on the basis of what he thinks he remembers. Therefore, it is not memory but imagination that engenders the novel. *A la Recherche du Temps Perdu* is not simply a work of fiction that looks backward to retrieve the past, it is above all a novel that looks forward towards its own future, towards its own making, as it reflects on its creative process. And that is also true of much of contemporary fiction, or what has been called New Fiction, Metafiction, Anti-fiction, Postmodern Fiction, or Surfiction.

Contemporary experimental fiction is no longer written as **remembered events**, but on the basis of **invented events** which seem to be happening (very much as in the cinema) right before the reader's eyes, in the present. This is a fundamental distinction, for it means that a writer need not turn to the past (his own past) to write fiction, but simply face the present or even the future. Yes, face the present or the future, thus no longer having to remember who or what he was or what he did, but instead inventing who or what he wants to be or have been or have done.

One of the great (autobiographical) novels of our time begins with a sentence that projects the reader (and the protagonist of the novel too) forward in time in order to be able to tell the story of the past: "*Many years later, as he faced the firing squad, Colonel Aureliano Buendia was to remember that distant afternoon when his father took him to discover ice.*"

What is amazing about the beginning of *One Hundred Years of Solitude* by Gabriel Garcia Marquez is that in order for the novel to be launched, in order for the story to be told, to be written in fact, the narrative must leap forward into the future before it can turn towards the past to recapture it. In this sense, it is no longer memory which controls the movement of the narrative, but imagination which functions as an improvisational instrument and makes the language of fiction progress. After all, we can only read a novel in one direction: forward and not backward.

Consequently, in much of contemporary fiction (even autobiographical fiction) imagination supersedes memory. That is why such fiction appears to be freely improvised rather than recounted. However, the fact that autobiographical avant-garde fiction becomes improvisational presents a paradox. It is indeed paradoxical for a novel to be called autobiographical and avant-garde at the same time, for these two terms exclude one another by their opposite functions, and therefore are contradictory. But then contemporary fiction delights in contradictions.

Conceptually, autobiography is a literary form that looks back to the past, whereas avant-garde fiction supposedly always looks forward. Autobiography attempts to recuperate past life in a retrospective narrative, avant-garde fiction invents new forms of narrative in order to precede, or even anticipate the future. This is why perhaps much of that fiction appears to be (at least on the surface) futuristic, explorative, or even science-fictional.

However, if the idea of autobiography and avant-garde fiction seems contradictory, the contradiction is often resolved by innovative techniques. Many contemporary writers use elements of their own life to create their fiction, but at the same time they undermine the credibility of these elements with irony, self-reflexiveness, authorial intrusions, and deliberate digressions and contradictions, and in so doing blur the line between facts and fiction, between the past, the present, and the future. That is true of my own novels, but it is also true of much of the fiction of Kurt Vonnegut Jr., William Burroughs, William T. Vollmann, but also Joseph McElroy in his novel *Plus*, Thomas Pynchon's *The Crying of Lot 49*, Italo Calvino's *Cosmicomics* and *T/Zero*, and even Samuel Beckett's *How It Is* and *The Lost Ones*, all of which can be read as futuristic works of fiction. In all these cases, even though autobiographical elements may be at work, the fiction reaches toward the future rather than the past. As such one could say that there exists today a kind of avant-garde autobiographical fiction, what Alain Robbe-Grillet calls, in reference to his own recent work, *La Nouvelle AutoBiographie.*

The combination of the past and the future in these experimental auto-biographical novels indicates a variety of changes in the relationship of art and life. On the one hand, these novels emphasize the close interaction of life and art in modern culture, and point to the increasingly impossible separation of fact and fiction. On the other hand, this changed nature of reality also implies the changed nature of narration as far as the conception of the self is concerned. This, of course, also affects the conventions of the novel, such as plot, setting, character, as well as the mimetic pretension of the traditional novel.

Probably the most interesting and most radical technique used to blur or even erase the line between fact and fiction is the intrusion of the author himself into the fiction, very often under his own name. This is the case with Kurt Vonnegut in *Slaughterhouse Five*, and in some of his other novels, who not only names himself as the author of the book but also as its protagonist. As such the real author is fictionalized as he inscribes himself in the text. Ronald Sukenick uses this same technique in all his novels, and consequently one can say that there is *a real Ronald Sukenick* but also *a mythical or fictional Ronald Sukenick*. Both share the same life, but both also share the same fiction. Which one is more true, more real than the other? That question can no longer be asked, for they both create each other mutually.

The fictitious author who appears in several of my novels is called FED-ERMAN (spelled either with a capital F or a small f). But that author is also known as HOMBRE DELLA PLUMA, HOMME DE PLUME, PEN-MAN, FEATHERMAN, or NAMREDEF. However, the fact of inscrib-ing one's name in one's fiction is only one way of subverting the factual and abolishing the boundary between reality and imagination— between the truth and the lie. Another way, even more effective, is self-reflexiveness, which points to the truth of fictitiousness while denounc-ing the imposture of realism. If it so happens that what is being told is drawn from the author's life, then it is undermined by self-reflexiveness.

Self-reflexive autobiographical fiction always speaks the truth about its own fraudulence, or rather denounces the lie of reality in order to assert the truth of fiction. And suddenly we are back in the LIAR'S PARADOX which states that, "*All writers are liars, I am a writer.*" But it is this para-dox which enables the fiction writer to transform the experiences of life into fiction and make these appear credible so that the reader can even-tually say: "*I may be suspicious of your life, but I trust your stories.*"

8. BEFORE POSTMODERNISM AND AFTER (PART 1)

> *You must have a little patience. I have undertaken, you see, to write not only my life but my opinions also; hoping and expecting that your knowledge of my character, and of what kind of a mortal I am (. . .) would give you a better relish of the other: As you proceed further with me, the slight acquaintance which is now beginning betwixt us, will grow into familiarity . . .*
>
> —Laurence Sterne

I. A NOSTALGIC RECONSIDERATION

Culture is a machine that backtracks into time, and art—literature especially—creates the past by transforming the present into unforgettable circumstances, that is to say circumstances that can be remembered, quoted, recited.

Preparing this presentation I faced an interesting decision: Should I speak of Postmodernism (and more specifically Postmodern fiction, since that is my subject) in the present tense or in the past tense?

Soon after the great Samuel Beckett died on December 22, 1989, a friend of mine wrote me in a letter of condolence: *Sam has now changed tense!*

Yes, perhaps Postmodernism also changed tense on December 22, 1989, with the death of Samuel Beckett—the first and the last Postmodern writer. The first: for if anyone can be said to have invented Postmodern fiction, it was certainly Samuel Beckett. *Murphy* and *Watt* are the first Postmodern novels. And Beckett was the last Postmodern writer because he was the last great artist of our time, the **last of the Mohicans**, as he was once called. *Stirrings Still* (*Soubresauts*, in French), the final work of Beckett, is also the last gasp of Postmodern fiction.

I cannot resist quoting a few lines from *Stirrings Still*, not only to prove what I have just said about Beckett, but especially because these lines may be the best illustration of how Postmodern fiction functioned:

> *But soon weary of vainly delving in those remains he moved on through the long hoar grass resigned to not knowing where he was or how he got there or where he was going or how to get back to whence he knew not how he came.*

As Beckett relentlessly demonstrated in his work, and once again at the end, with this remarkable piece of syntax: the search for the means to put an end to things—an end to language, an end to literature—is what enabled the Postmodern discourse to perpetuate itself.

There is in *Stirrings Still* (inscribed in the title as well as in the entire text, and clearly demonstrated by the passage I just quoted) the simultaneous affirmation of two incompatible and contradictory conditions: movement and immobility. Yes, there is in this final Beckett text a **moving immobility**. To stir, of course, means to move. The term **stirrings** supposes that there is **still** movement. But the term **still** (ambiguous as it is here) implies immobility. On the one hand then, an affirmation of movement, on the other the declaration of non-movement.

This contradictory condition of movement and immobility, words and silence, wandering and internment, was the basis on which the entire oeuvre of Samuel Beckett was founded, but I would venture to affirm, that this contradictory condition of **moving immobility** (this **aporia**, as Beckett was fond of calling it) was fundamental to the making and the unmaking of Postmodernism.

If *Stirrings Still* (Beckett's last words) speaks of death, it is not, however, the type of death which transforms final words into a testament. It speaks, as Beckett did for fifty years, of this supreme indecision which gathers in itself all contradictions without deluding them. This, I believe, is what Postmodernism was all about: **A Supreme Indecision!**

I am writing today about **The End of Postmodernism,** which to me also means **The Death of Postmodernism.** In other words, I am in the process of burying Postmodernism . . .

But Postmodernism was an honorable activity. Many of us survived on it, and so rather than rejoice because we finally got rid of this cumbersome term, we should perhaps deplore the end of Postmodernism. After all, for some of us, who at one time or another were involved in fabricating Postmodern fiction, it was fun while it lasted. And I have fond memories of some of the Postmodern gatherings to which I was invited. Ah the wild Postmodern evenings of wine tasting in Würzburg, the wild Postmodern poker games in Milwaukee, the wild Postmodern intellectual and social orgies in Buffalo, and in so many other exotic places! Yes, I have fond memories of all these wild Postmodern happenings. And so, before leaving Postmodernism behind, we should perhaps ask, for the last time: What was it? What made it possible? What political, social, aesthetic conditions so radically transformed the writing of fiction during the past four decades or so?

Yes, **before** exploring the **aftermath** of Postmodernism—the "New Directions" of Postmodernism (as these are now the topics of many conferences in many parts of the world), we should perhaps talk about the **before** of Postmodernism.

However, even though my fiction has often been labeled Postmodern, and I have read many books written about Postmodernism (for I am vain enough to search in every book for the mention of my name, but sardonic enough to mock my own eagerness), quite frankly I have never understood what Postmodernism was. Or as Beckett's Unnamable once put it: *To tell the truth, let us be honest at least, it is some considerable time now since I last knew what I was talking about.*

In fact, I believe that no one really knew what Postmodernism was, except, perhaps, Ihab Hassan (who invented not only the term Postmodernism, in spite of what others may claim, but watched over it for many years, until Postmodernism took the wrong turn). Yes, I do not think that those writers who were labeled Postmodern ever understood what it was, what it meant, how it functioned, and yet continued to produce works of fiction which were truly Postmodern. But now that the entire world, the entire universe for that matter has become Postmodern, these writers can now stand back and watch, with some degree of amusement, the consequences of what they set in motion some years ago.

Yes, the entire Universe has become Postmodern. A *Newsweek* article about astronomy used the term Postmodern to describe the strange behavior of certain cosmic bodies in the galaxies, and recently I saw an advertisement in a glossy fashion magazine describing an evening gown as being Postmodern, and I understand that McDonald's and Burger King are furiously competing to produce the first Postmodern Hamburger. And didn't we watch just a year or so ago the first Postmodern War specially made for television, played in the present tense twenty-four hours a day, and now available for replay on video tape from CNN for $24.95? But that's not all. Here is an inventory of cultural items which have been described as Postmodern. I found that list on page 139 of a collection of essays, just published in England, entitled *Postmodernism and Contemporary Fiction* (edited by Edmund J. Smyth).

postmodern now

The décor of a room, the design of a building, the diagesis of a film, the making of a Rock and Roll disk or an MTV video tape, a television commercial or a documentary, the intertextual relations between a television commercial and a documentary, the layout of a page in a fashion magazine or a critical journal, space capsules, the anti-teleological tendency within epistemology, cold dark matter, the attack on the metaphysics of presence, the general attenuation of feelings in Mankind, the collective chagrin and morbid projections of the postwar generation of Baby-boomers confronting the disillusionment of middle-age, the predicament of reflexivity **(but not mentioned the irritation of self-reflexiveness)**, the stubbornness of rhetorical tropes, the proliferation of surfaces, the new phase in commodity fetishism, the fascination for images, codes and styles, political or existential fragmentation, the decentering of the subject, the replacement of unitary power axes by a plurality of power formations, the implosion of meaning, the collapse of cultural hierachies, the dread engendered by the threat of nuclear destruction, the decline of the university, endangered animal species, the functioning and effects of the new miniaturized technologies, the sense of placelessness or the abandonment of placelessness (depending on who you read), and so on.

I skipped a few, and added a few, but the one thing missing from this list is Postmodern fiction, and that is interesting. For now that Postmodernism has taken over all human and animal activities, and in the process those of us who inadvertently created Postmodern works of fiction have been forgotten, or relegated to the zone of nonbeing, it may be the right time for us to look back and consider, reconsider calmly what we did, how we did it, and why we did it?

II. THE MIGRATION OF POSTMODERN FICTION

A screaming comes across the sky. It has happened before, but there is nothing to compare it to now. These are, of course, the opening words of *Gravity's Rainbow*.

Indeed, like a screaming across the sky, Postmodern fiction came and went, and *there is nothing to compare it to now*. It passed by, overhead, and even by-passed us. But then that is true of all avant-garde movements: to by-pass and be by-passed. All great avant-garde movements never have time to finish what they set out to accomplish. Postmodern fiction was also interrupted.

It is true, though, that an avant-garde movement can never, and should never achieve its purpose, otherwise it ceases to be avant-garde. By its very nature, that of opposing or rejecting established modes of creation, an avant-garde movement is destined to tentativeness and unfinishedness. That is the paradox of avant-gardism. Struggling within the confines of self-reflexive orientation, the avant-garde bears curious witness to an ambiguous state of mind. It displays a creative and critical vitality, yet raises only minimal expectations. Its most significant innovations involve the self-conscious exploration of the nature, limits, and possibilities of art. But the vision of the future that avant-garde art provides is always tentative and unclear, as if unable to see beyond doubt and distrust.

That was true of Postmodern fiction too: it could not see beyond doubt and distrust, but at the same time it made of doubt and distrust an occasion, and that was its strength.

Other movements (not necessarily avant-garde) always interrupt what is in progress. Cubism interrupted Impressionism, Constructivism put an end to Cubism, Surrealism negated Dadaism, Structuralism displaced Existentialism, and so on. What is not clear so far, however, is what interrupted Postmodernism? Certainly not the uninspired Minimalist K-Mart Fiction of the last decade, nor Cyberpunk Fiction, nor Hi-Tech Fiction, nor Sudden Fiction, nor Illuminated Fiction, nor Transfiction, or whatever term qualifies fiction these days on the covers of anthologies.

No, Postmodern fiction was not killed by any of these things, it simply came and went like a flock of migratory birds, and we followed its flight across the sky, and watched it disappear over the horizon. Out of a strange necessity, but above all because it carried in itself its own demise (epistemological and ontological doubt conveyed through disjointed formal structures) Postmodernism had to either die or go elsewhere and become something else, which is what it did, even though it continues to be called by the same name.

In this sense, by contemplating its own demise and its own impossibility, Postmodern fiction may, after all, have met John Gardner's criteria for **Moral Fiction**: *true moral fiction*, wrote John Gardner some years ago, *is an experiment too difficult and dangerous to try in the World, but safe and important in the mirror image of reality in the writer's mind.*

Certainly death must be the example *par excellence* of something *too difficult and dangerous to try in the world*. Postmodern fiction experimented with **death**, or rather with its **own death**. It won. Like a screaming . . . no, better yet, like a ghost it passed across the sky, for it is clear from all the discussion still going on today about Postmodernism that a pantheon is in the process of being constructed for it, however reluctantly.

When I was a boy in Paris, quite a few years ago, and a plane passed overhead in the sky, everyone would rush out into the street to follow its flight. Pointing to the sky with one finger we would all shout with a tone of wonderment: *Regarde, regarde, un avion . . . Oh, comme c'est beau!* But I think we were also wondering: How the hell does it stay up there?

Postmodernism is (was) that plane! How the hell did it manage to survive its own death for four decades?

In one of those so-called Postmodern novels, entitled *The Twofold Vibration*, one of the characters tells an other: *You have found a way to make your past live by pointing to its grave with your finger and of course we can't catch you at it, it's just a motion, a gesture, a clever substitution, and this way you put all your guilt on others, on us, but the fact that you choose to speak about it, even evasively, and write about it too, is that transcendence or escape?*

To which, the other character replies: *Yes, that's exactly the problem, exactly what my life is all about, and my writing too, escape or transcendence, you've put your finger right on it, though I would say more escaping than transcending.*

I think Postmodern fiction was exactly that: both an escape and a transcendence.

III. THE PREMATURE DEATH OF POSMODERNISM

Did I say that Postmodernism died on December 22, 1989, when Samuel Beckett changed tense? That was only the final gasp. Postmodernism started dying at the very moment it was born (whatever date one ascribes to that moment) and continued dying when such figures as Vladimir Nabokov, Michel Foucault, Roland Barthes, Georges Perec, Julio Cortazar, Jorge Luis Borges, Italo Calvino, John Coltrane (I include that name to remind us that John Coltrane's type of jazz was also Postmodern), Donald Barthelme, Thomas Bernhard, and not too long ago Jerzy Kosinski, and others, many others I have forgotten, also changed tense, most of them prematurely. Postmodernism was a long list of names—a great many now absent, though a few stubborn ones are still present.

But Postmodernism was also Abstract Expressionism, Le Nouveau Roman, Structuralism, Post-Structuralism, Semiotics, rediscovered Russian Formalism, Conceptualism, Deconstruction, Metafiction, Antifiction, Surfiction, New Journalism, and even Rock and Roll as Larry McCaffery convincingly demonstrated in a recent essay, in *The American Book Review*.

However, all these names, all these terms suddenly seem so dated—passé and dépassé—and yet, somehow I have a vague feeling that we never knew what happened. Yes, something happened, but we don't know what. Postmodernism by-passed us in a flash, and we still have not come to terms with it.

Having come to **The End of Postmodernism,** and at the same time the end of Postmodern Fiction, at least we now have a chance for a new beginning, and so in the spirit of perpetual beginnings, it might be good to remember that story of Robert Coover that opens with a writer who in order to get started shoots himself. His blood hits the wall and spells out this message: *It is important to begin when everything is already over.*

This does not mean that I am proposing we all commit suicide immediately, but the death of Postmodernism may have given us the possibility of a new beginning, the chance for a rebirth. Have we learned anything? Perhaps we should go back and reread that incredible passage near the end of *Malone Dies* [yes, Beckett again] where Old Malone who earlier on had said, *I shall die without enthusiasm,* somehow manages to outwit and outlive his own death by being reborn (in a manner of speaking) into death. Here is that passage:

> *All is ready. Except me. I am being given, if I may venture the expression, birth to into death, such is my impression. The feet are clear already, of the great cunt of existence. Favorable presentation I trust. My head will be last to die. Haul in your hands. I can't. The render rent. My story ended, I'll be living yet. Promising lag. That is the end of me. I shall say I no more.*

This was written circa 1949. But of course Malone, or whatever name the Beckett creature invented for itself, continued to die for another forty years.

There may not be any **New** discernible **Directions** yet at **The End of Postmodernism,** but there is certainly the possibility of a new beginning. Let us take advantage of this opportunity.

And who knows, perhaps we are already in this new beginning. Or to paraphrase John Barth at the beginning of *Sabbatical* (I'm sure he won't mind the slight alteration): *We* would be happy to give it another go; we have fiddled *[long enough]* with our tale through this whole *[postmodern]* sabbatical voyage.

———————

Back in 1974, at a Postmodern conference, or rather I should say, a conference on Postmodern fiction, in Milwaukee by the way, an antagonistic critic drew a line on the blackboard and explained to the audience that this straight line represented the history of narrative from its beginning to its end . . .

DIGRESSION: Had Samuel Beckett been present, he would probably have added, with a touch of irony, remembering **The Lost Ones:** from its *unthinkable* beginning to its *impossible* end.

Then the critic drew a small deviation in the line, a little loop, and turning to the captive audience that had assembled on that day either to accept or reject Postmodern fiction (in those days, one was **for or against** everything), he continued to explain that this deviation was the Postmodern moment, that for some unexplained reasons narrative had deviated from its course, from the norm, and that it was happening now (in November 1974—yes, I think it was November) . . . there was restlessness in the audience when he said that . . . but the professor-critic in question, whose name shall not be revealed here, quickly added: *But do not worry, do not despair, soon the line will redress itself and continue on its straight course.* He paused, stroked his academic beard, with obvious self-satisfaction, sneered, and added slowly, detaching each syllable: *That-is i-ne-vi-ta-ble.* I suppose he could have added, *Because It is Written Above,* as it is said again and again (but with irony, of course) in one of the great pre-postmodern novels of all times, *Jacques le Fataliste,* by Denis Diderot.

A sigh of relief was heard and felt in the auditorium.

And indeed, the straight line of narrative may have found the right and righteous path again. But something did happen, something changed. What are left now are the traces of that strange and radical activity known as Postmodernism. Traces of a discourse (**A Real Fictitious Discourse,** I once called it) which took shape during the past four decades and then deconstructed itself. It is of this discourse, that I want to speak for a few moments. To do this I shall turn to what I know best, my own real fictitious discourse.

IV. THE ERA OF SUSPICION

When the Writer, the Penman, L'Homme de Plume, or to speak more openly and personally, when Federman sat down on October 1, 1966 (he was in Paris then, spending the year thanks to a generous Guggenheim fellowship to write, supposedly, a scholarly book about **New Trends in Contemporary French Poetry,** of which there were none), when Federman sat down on October 1, 1966, to write the first sentence of *Double or Nothing* (his first novel—first published novel) . . .

That first sentence goes like this: *Once upon a time (two or three weeks ago), a rather stubborn and determined middle-aged man decided to record for posterity . . . and so on . . .*

When, I was saying, Federman sat down to write that first sentence curious things were happening around him in the world, and especially in the world of letters.

Marshall McLuhan had just declared the end of the printed word. The French Structuralists had announced the death of the author. My late friend Jacques Ehrmann (who introduced Structuralism at Yale, with the controversial 1966 issues of *Yale French Studies,* and perhaps inadvertently started the whole Postmodern mess in America) published a book in Paris entitled *La Mort de la Littérature.* Still in France, Les Nouveaux Romanciers and Les Nouveaux Nouveaux Romanciers of the Tel Quel Group were caught in what Nathalie Sarraute called in a collection of essays by that title, *L'Ère du Soupçon* (The Era of Suspicion). Meanwhile, back in America, Professor Ronald Sukenick then teaching at Cornell University was announcing to his students the death of the novel while writing at the same time a story entitled **The Death of the Novel,** and in Buffalo, John Barth was finishing the first draft of his now famous essay, **The Literature of Exhaustion,** while trying to work his way out of the labyrinthine **Funhouse** of fiction. And many others in many other places **(In the Heart of the Heart of the Country)** at about the same time were also lamenting (in speaking or in writing) the death of the novel, the death of the author, the end of literature.

It was in this climate, this funerary climate, surrounded by such negative conditions, confronting all these apocalyptic predictions that the fiction writer, in the mid-sixties, considered his task and began writing his new novel. Obviously, his work could only be marked by doubt and distrust, but especially self-doubt, which, however, the stubborn but clever writer, who faced at the same time the impossibility and the necessity of writing, quickly turned to his advantage by transforming it into self-reflexiveness, which for a while, at least, helped him survive so he could continue to destroy the novel that he was in the process of writing.

It was by doubting history, society, politics, culture, as well as his own art, which of course also meant doubting the historical discourse, the political discourse, the literary discourse, and so on, that the writer somehow managed to do his work. That writer even went as far as doubting the reality of reality.

But then all great movements—philosophical, religious, political or artistic—always begin with doubt. For instance:

> *There is no novelty to me in the reflection that, from my earlier years, I have accepted many false opinions as true, and that what I have concluded from such badly assured premises could not but be highly doubtful and uncertain. From the time that I first recognized this fact, I have realized that if I wished to have any firm and constant knowledge [. . .] I would have to undertake, once and for all, to set aside all the opinions which I had previously accepted among my beliefs and start again from the very beginning.*

In this case, however, the writer did not shoot himself, as the writer in Robert Coover's story did, in order to be able to begin, but instead he continued his meditation **Concerning Things That Can Be Doubted.**

What I have just quoted is not from a Postmodern novel, but the opening lines of the *First Meditation* of René Descartes. Whom I now officially declare a Postmodern writer.

But let's take a more recent example of a work of fiction launched by doubt—that of Ronald Sukenick who begins his story, *The Death of the Novel*, this way:

> *The contemporary writer—the writer who is acutely in touch with the life of which he is part—is forced to start from scratch: Reality doesn't exist, time doesn't exist, personality doesn't exist. God was the omniscient author, but he died; now no one knows the plot, and since our reality lacks the sanction of a creator, there is no guarantee as to the authenticity of the received version.*

Doubting the authenticity of the received version, whether factual or fictitious, it was with a deep sense of doubt and suspicion in what fiction was still capable of doing, that the writer (Federman, in this case) set out to write *Double or Nothing* on October 1, 1966—a novel which sustained itself by conquering doubt on every page with *typographical laughter* (to use Ihab Hassan's expression). But let me assure you, The Penman was not trying to write a Postmodern novel, or even an experimental novel, when he started *Double or Nothing*, he was just trying to write **a novel** out of a personal necessity, in the face of the impossibility of writing a novel.

Self-doubt, even fear that the game might be too difficult, might even be impossible, hovered over the postmodern narrative. But the self-doubt of the writer/gambler became an expression of the fiction's own doubt. The game, for it was a game, in effect, was not just a device, a definition, or a celebration, it was also a necessity—the means to inch the story forward, page by page, to get the story told despite the fierce self-doubt that plagued the writer. In the end, the story did get told (**The Death of the Novel** engendered **Other Stories**), and the telling that digressed from the telling or that cancelled itself was in fact the triumph of Postmodern fiction. The anxiety of the telling, at least for the sustained moment of the book, had been overcome, even though along the way character, plot, setting, and all the other conventions of fiction were transformed or destroyed. The beginning had succeeded in reaching an ending, even though by miscalculation. Suddenly the Postmodern story was finished, ready to die, so that it could, however, be resurrected, in some other time and some other place.

What the new story will be, I cannot tell, yet, but perhaps others will be able to tell us. Meanwhile, as the first and last Postmodern writer once put it: *I don't know why I told this story. I could just as well have told another. Perhaps some other time I'll be able to tell another.* [Samuel Beckett, of course].

Meanwhile, at the same time in some other places (we are back in the mid-sixties), others were also writing books with doubt in their minds, and even panic in their bodies, books which eventually were published under these revealing titles: *Killing Time, Death Kit, The Ticket That Exploded, Unspeakable Practices Unnatural Acts, Willie Master's Lonesome Wife, Up, Lunar Landscapes, Slaughterhouse Five, Quake, Nuclear Love,*

Mumbo Jumbo, In Cold Blood, The Exagggeration of Peter Prince [yes, with three g's], *The Last Gentleman, The Crying of Lot 49, Lost in the Funhouse* . . .

The titles of these works of fiction, all of them published between 1966 and 1968, are indicative of the anxiety inscribed in the texts. Looking back at these books (novels, collections of stories), all of them ultimately declared Postmodern, however different one from the other, they all seem to have been written with a deep sense of doubt and distrust—about where and when they were written, about themselves, and about what they were attempting to do.

DOUBT is indeed the term that best explains and defines Postmodern fiction. Founded on doubt and perpetuating itself with doubt, the fiction written in the 1960s and 1970s not only doubted itself, but it also doubted the historical and cultural conditions in which it was created. The results were fascinating, though often irritating to many.

For it is true that in the past thirty years or so, literature went through a time of radical disturbances that totally overturned the institution and its primary values.

In a world where the referential element itself was denounced as a mystifying electronic image, the old question of historical (and literary) truth and credibility, as well as the question of the stability of the real, were no longer valid. These became impossible questions. Because the historical and the literary discourses were falsified by their own language, all referential coherence became irrelevant and even derisive. The institution of literature never recovered.

The repeated announcements of the death of literature during the sixties, and the way Postmodernism went about demonstrating that death, during the next two decades, led Leslie Fiedler, the great advocate of **pop-lit** who was delighted to see high-brow literature go under, to write, in the eighties, a book entitled *What Was Literature*.

And it is also true that internally, the traditional romantic and modernist literary values were completely reversed during the Postmodern era. The author, whose creative imagination was said to be the source of literature, was declared dead or the mere assembler of various bits of language and culture into writings that were no longer works of

art but simply cultural collages or **texts**. As a result Postmodern literature could no longer produce original works of art **(masterpieces)**, nor
could it have great artists **(masters)**, it could only produce works which
resembled one another, and writers who mostly imitated each other's
work. In fact, many authors themselves shamelessly admitted to being
mere plagiarizers. The great historical tradition extending from Homer
to the present was broken up in discontinuous fragments. The influence of earlier writers on their successors was declared no longer bene-
ficial but the source of anxiety and weakness. Certain Postmodern writers even went as far as claiming to have influenced their predecessors. It
was even said that *Don Quixote* could not have been written without the
influence of Postmodernism.

The literary canon was analyzed, debated, and eventually dismantled,
while literary history itself was discarded as a diachronic illusion, to be
replaced by a synchronic paradigm. Masterpieces of literature were
now void of meaning, or, what comes to the same thing, filled with an
excess of meaning, their language indeterminate, contradictory, without
any foundation, their organization, structures, grammar, logic, and
rhetoric, mere verbal performances. Whatever meaning these masterpieces may have had was simply provisional and conferred on them by
the reader, not inherent in the text or set in place for all time by the
writer's craft. Rather than being near-sacred myths of human experience
of the world and the self, the most prized possessions of culture, universal statements about an unchanging and essential human nature,
literature was increasingly treated as authoritarian and destructive of
human freedom, the ideology of patriarchy devised to serve white male
supremacy over the female and lesser breeds. Criticism, which was
once the scorned servant of literature, declared its independence and
insisted that it too was literature.

Of course, not everyone accepted these new views—twisted views as
they were called—but gradually they became the reality of the moment.
It is clear now that these transformations were the results of what happened when (once upon a time, not too long ago) Postmodernism displaced Modernism.

Those opposed to Postmodernism called that situation a crisis. For
instance, George Steiner (in *Real Presences*, 1989), describes the crisis
of Western intellectual life of the past three decades or so as being
fully inhabited by what he calls *the nostalgia, pathos, and failure of*

consolation that constitutes modernity itself (but of course, by **modernity** he really means **postmodernity**).

That crisis, Steiner argues, is the unprecedented transformation of *the fecund confrontation of intelligence with the facticity of death, a facticity wholly resistant to reason, to metaphor, to revelatory representation.* For Steiner (and others who think like him) aesthetic forms are inhabited by transcendental values—values that refer beyond the time and place of their articulations—and the crisis of our time is the failure to discern an intelligible order within temporal human existence. In an age of the instantaneous, such as the Postmodern age, the possibility of transcendental values seems to Steiner to be irrevocably lost. In such an age, the *acceptance of ephemerality and self-dissolution embodies the underlying nihilistic findings of incomprehension.*

Depending on which side of Postmodernism one stands, and how one feels about the intellectual situation of the past three decades or so, one can interpret Steiner's views either negatively or positively.

For myself, being an incurable optimist, I will simply conclude part 1 of this presentation by repeating that **even though some people might say that the Postmodern situation was not very encouraging one must reply that it was not meant to encourage those who say that.**

[I cannot remember if I wrote this
or if I read it]

BEFORE POSTMODERNISM
AND AFTER (PART 2)

I started part 1 of this paper in the middle of a quotation, I will start part 2 also in the middle of a quotation, and I will probably finish this presentation in the middle of another quotation. For, as we know from having lived and studied Postmodernism, quotations were central and essential to its existence. It was by leaping from quotation to quotation (known as The Leap-Frog Technique—see *Take It or Leave It*, by Raymond Federman) and often even by quoting itself (known as **inter-textuality**, but which I prefer to call **incest-tuality**), that the Postmodern text progressed without really going anywhere, thus delaying or even at times cancelling its own end—its own eventual death.

A quotation is, of course, the repetition of something already said or written. As such it adds nothing new to what is in the process of being said or written. It merely gives the illusion of amplification, of enlargement, of progress.

But in fact, a text built on quotations (regardless of whether these come from an external or an internal source) cannot go forward, cannot advance; it can only backtrack into time or into itself. Therefore, one could say of the Postmodern text, what Diderot once confessed about himself: *I listen only for the pleasure of repeating*. And so, here is the quotation that will give the second part of this presentation the illusion of going somewhere.

> *These few general remarks to begin with. What am I to do, what shall I do, what should I do, in my situation, how proceed? By* **aporia** *pure and simple? Or by affirmations and negations invalidated as uttered—or*

*sooner or later? Generally speaking. There must be other shifts? Otherwise it would be quite hopeless. But it is quite hopeless. I should mention before going any further, any further on, that I say **aporia** without knowning what it means.*

These general remarks were pronounced by The Unnamable at the beginning of Beckett's novel by that title. [Yes, Beckett again, the first and last Postmodern writer, as I declared earlier]. These general remarks summarize, I believe, the dilemma of Postmodernism. Or what I called in part 1: **the supreme indecision** of Postmodernism. From its beginning to its end—*by affirmations and negations invalidated as utterred*—Postmodernism questioned itself as to how to proceed? As a late Postmodernist (late in the sense of belonging to a movement which has already departed), I seem to have a similar problem here. How to proceed beyond **Postmodernism,** beyond what is in the process of finishing—of dying? Well, obviously, by leaping from quotation to quotation.

Therefore, let us leap-frog to **The End of Postmodernism!**

Preparing this essay, some months ago, I wrote a letter to twenty of my friends (writers, critics, professors, entertainers) asking them to answer these two questions:

 1. Do you think Postmodernism is dead?
 2. If so, what killed it?

To my great delight, all twenty correspondents replied, but all asked not to be identified. These are the twenty answers I received:

 1. Postmodernism was an exercise in discontinuity, rupture, break, mutation, transformation, therefore doomed from the beginning . . .
 2. As with all new things, once absorbed by the economy Postmodernism was finished . . .
 3. Now that the effects of Postmodernism are evident in sectors as diverse as dress, food, and lodging, and are in those forms understood, the end is not far . . .
 4. Postmodernism began as a genuine if loose literary movement and ended as a department store curiosity . . .
 5. When the academy starts to take sides and quibbles about Postmodernism, it quickly kills what it discusses . . .
 6. In winning the day, Postmodernism, of course, loses . . .

7. Because Postmodernism was viewed both as a movement and a perfume, and both as an intellectual disposition and a bowl of fruit, it had no chance to survive . . .

8. Postmodernism as a literary notion was invented to deal with the Holocaust. The prewar split between form and content was incapable of dealing with the moral crisis provoked by the Holocaust, and therefore writers like Beckett, Walter Abish, Ronald Sukenick, Primo Levi, Raymond Federman, Jerzy Kosinski, and many others, invented Postmodernism to search among the dead, to dig into the communal grave, in order to re-animate wasted blood and wasted tears . . . or perhaps simply in order **to create something more interesting than death** (as Claude Lanzman did in *Shoah*, for instance— one of the great Postmodern films).

9. When something completes its intellectual and moral journey it is enshrined within sealed cases in the various Sorbonnes, like the relics of saints, and is venerated in much the same way and with the same useless result, and so it is with Posmodernism . . .

10. When among critics the tone of the debate shifts from intellectual to moral, then we know that Posmodernism is dead . . .

11. The death of anything is, of course, a trope not for its death but for its utility, its applicability. Now Postmodernism no longer avails, no longer applies . . .

12. When a movement becomes a choice and not a necessity, as Postmodernism has now become, it signifies its death. But since one can never speak one's death in the present—one's death can only be spoken by others after it happens—the death of Postmodernism is now being spoken by everyone, everywhere . . .

13. The central, fundamental literary texts of Postmodernism: *Texts For Nothing, The Library of Babel, Cosmicomics, Lost in the Funhouse, The Voice in the Closet.* These texts announced and performed the end of Postmodernism while pretending to serve as its beginning . . .

14. The current reactionary literary climate dominated by works in received forms does not indicate the death of Postmodernism as much as the persistence of the power of market economies to define the arts . . .

15. Literary fashions have more to do with the reception of literature than with its creation, and therefore more to do with its end than its beginning . . .

16. While it is true that the current literary scene viewed from a certain perspective looks sterile, it is more true that it is extraordinarily fallow, ready to submit, ready to compromise, in a quiveringly recep-

tive mode. Postmodernism died because it refused to compromise . . .

17. When the great painters of New York City (Stella, Johns, Rauchenberg, etc.) went to work for *Women's Wear Daily*, as they did en masse in 1960, the end was at hand (the visual arts always lead, the literary arts follow). The death of Postmodernism was sealed in 1960, the same year it was born . . .

18. The great works of any age always spring from a personal necessity that is only subsequently elaborated into this or that theory and chiefly as a means of publicizing said great works. Theory killed Postmodernism, but the irony is that theory was also Postmodernism . . .

19. Postmodernism was responding to the end—the end of Europe, after World War II. Just as Modernism, earlier, responded to the breakdown of self-evident truths (the consistency of truth, one might say) elaborated during the nineteenth century, Postmodernism cried and decried nothingness, nonsense, and death, and in so doing cried and decried its own nothingness, nonsense and death . . .

20. It isn't, to say it again, that Posmodernism is dead but like any other identifiable phenomenon of a certain value—such as Impressionism, Dadaism, Surrealism, Modernism, Abstract Expressionism, New Criticism, Feminism—after a fixed period of bubbling at the surface, it sinks and recombines with other like elements to form again a part of the generative stew of art and culture, and that moment of rot is called the death of a movement . . .

The general sense one gets from these replies (some quite fascinating, I think) is that Postmodernism is indeed dead, **finished**: on the one hand because it was swallowed and digested by the economy and eventually excreted and disseminated into the culture, on the other hand because it was stifled by academic bickering and consequently turned into a futile debate (especially in America).

Now some people might say that this situation is not very encouraging but one must reply that it is not meant to encourage those who say that.

Oops, I think I've already said that, in Part 1, and other places too. Oh well, like all good Postmodernists, I suffer of intertextuality and repetition.

But one could ask, to continue in the questioning mode: Why did Post-modernism allowed itself to be swallowed and digested by the culture, or to be stifled by academic theorizing?

And the answer would be: **Because Postmodernism, and more specifically Postmodern fiction, moved from continuity, from fluidity, coherence, linearity (in history as well as in literature) to discontinuity, fragmentation, indeterminacy, plurality, metafictionality, intertextuality, decentering, dislocation, ludism, to become series of disconnected states, combinations of impulses, incoherent lists and verbal doodles, it eventually destroyed itself.**

But, one could also ask, isn't literature language? And isn't language always stable? **Yes, of course, literature is made of language, but language limited by the permutations of a restricted number of elements and functions. However, what made Postmodern fiction interesting and important, and vulnerable too, is that it tried to escape these restrictions, it tried to say what is beyond language, that is why Postmodern fiction was doomed from the beginning. Even though the unspeakable can never be spoken, Postmodernism attempted to speak the impossibility of speaking the unspeakable.**

But isn't literature an invention, and as such can it not invent its own language? [My imaginary questioner is very stubborn]. **No, literature is always a reinvention, it never creates anything new, it simply reinvents the nothing new, in other words—just as the sun every day, having no alternative, rises on the nothing new. Postmodern fiction only reinvented what had been banished, hidden, or expelled from individual or collective memory, this is why it was accused of being plagiaristic, and of working Against Itself.**

DIGRESSION: Allow me to clarify this last statement with another quotation, this time from *L'Entretien Infini* by Maurice Blanchot: *To write is always first to rewrite, and to rewrite does not mean to revert to a previous form of writing, no more than to an anteriority of speech, or of presence, or of meaning. To rewrite is a form of undoubling which always precedes unity, or suspends it while plagiarizing it.* [My translation] [End of Digression]

But isn't literature independent of its author? **Literature may pretend to be independent of the personality of its author, but it is always about** some profound (subconscious) obsession of the author and of the society in which he lives. This was particularly true of Postmodern Fiction.

But isn't literature always a form of orientation? Literature either confirms, accepts, supports, defends the status quo, or else questions, challenges, denounces, rejects the status quo. Whatever the case, orientation presupposes a disorientation, and that is exactly what Postmodernism did: it disoriented.

But isn't the spirit in which one writes decisive in exerting a critical response? The boundary between writing and reading is not always clearly marked. The spirit in which one read Postmodern fiction was often decisive in exerting a negative critical response. But as Roland Barthes pointed out in *The Pleasure of the Text*, *the author cannot choose to write what will not be read in his book.*

These are the reasons why the Postmodern writer was, in fact, different—different and therefore disorienting to most by that difference. The Postmodern writer understood that at the heart of the heart of his otherness, he had a right to his difference, to his way of seeing and writing the world, however confused and confusing that world may have been.

To write fiction during the Postmodern era [I would like to remind you that I am still speaking of Postmodernism in the past tense] was above all an effort to create a DIFFERENCE (or *DIFFÉRANCE*, with an **A** as Jacques Derrida spelled it), and not continue to pretend that fiction was the same—the same as reality.

If there seems to be a contradiction here in terms of what I said earlier about Postmodern fiction being mere repetition, or reinvention of the already said or written, it is because the Postmodern difference I am trying to point to here, was not a difference of subject or of subject-matter, but a difference of process—process of telling, of **presenting** rather than **re-presenting**. That is why the originality of convention in Postmodern fiction grew more and more absolute and arbitrary, for invention consisted in devising new sets of rules by which the familiar pieces could be rearranged. For to play the same old game by the same old rules would have been mere competence, rather than artistry.

If traditional realistic fiction was a representation of **the same**, Postmodern fiction was a presentation of **difference**—a liberation of what was different. **And what was different was the difference.** Or as the Postmodern reincarnation of Scheherazade explained in *Chimera*: *It's as if—as if the key to the treasure is the treasure.*

Reflecting on the contemporary discourse (circa 1970) Michel Foucault wrote: *In order to liberate difference we must have a contradictory thought, free of dialectic, free of negation. A thought which says yes to divergence; an affirmative thought, whose instrument is disjunction; a thought of the multiple; a thought which does not obey a scholarly model, but which addresses insoluble problems with **a play of repetition**.* [My translation]

As good a definition of Postmodern fiction as any. For paradoxically, by playing with repetition Postmodern fiction created a difference, a difference which negated all claims of adequacy to the natural or to the true.

As such, Postmodern fiction offered itself as a playful object, and even as an object of pleasure, a toy, a game with which the reader was asked to play. One needs only to reread Donald Barthelme's *Snow White*, John Barth's *Lost in the Funhouse*, Steve Katz's *Creamy and Delicious*, Robert Coover's *Spanking the Maid*, and so on, to see, to feel, how Postmodern fiction offered itself as a toy, a game, an object of pleasure. Or as Roland Barthes so joyfully demonstrated in the *Pleasure of the Text*, Postmodern fiction found a way to speak pleasure—no! even better than that, found a way to exult bliss.

Of course, not everyone is willing to be discomforted or unsettled by a **Postmodern text of bliss.** Allan Bloom (a critic who has probably never known *jouissance*) in *The Closing of the American Mind* dismisses Postmodernism when he tells us that *Not a single book of lasting importance was produced in or around that movement.* According to him, the Postmodern writer was infected with relativism, believing that all values are only opinions, and one opinion as good as another, and therefore this misguided writer lived in a daze of universal tolerance, apathy, blasphemy, and ignorance. Whether or not Allan Bloom is correct is quite irrelevant. A large and fascinating body of Postmodern fiction is still present today and still in need of serious evaluation. What is disturbing to Allan Bloom is that Postmodern fiction depicted a reality that he prefers to deny—a confused reality, certainly, but a depiction of it that is a far more accurate delineation of quotidian existence than the illusions of reality devised by the writers of the 30's and 40's, or the retreating neo-realists of the 80's, or the virtual realists now emerging in the nineties.

It is the likes of Allan Bloom who put an end to Postmodernism, or displaced it to some other cultural region to become an inoffensive topic of *cacademic* debates. By disguising his argument for the preservation of what one might term the **comfortable familiar** as a reference for an indisputable paradigm, Allan Bloom is able to dismiss four decades of astonishing radical literary activities.

And he is not alone in this. There are many *fools of all kinds, these days, who have decreed foreclosure of the text and of its pleasure* [I am quoting Roland Barthes here], *either by cultural conformism or by intransigent rationalism or by political moralism or by criticism of the signifier or by stupid pragmatism or by snide vacuity or by destruction of the discourse, loss of verbal desire.*

E. Donald Hirsch's trivial list of requisites for a properly informed culture, Robert Richman's desperate call for a revival of good old-fashioned literature, William Bennett's demand for a return to the basics of education are all symptoms of a last stand, a tightening of the circle of wagons against the attack of the Postmodern barbarians upon the **comfortable familiar**. All these **fools** (as Roland Barthes calls them) are begging for the preservation of **sameness** against **difference**.

What Allan Bloom and all those who think like him want is to be told, re-told, what they already know. In other words, they want to be comforted in their knowledge. This is why they must oppose or dismiss all innovative activities, all experimentations which discomfort (*perhaps to the point of a certain boredom*). Postmodern fiction certainly made many of its readers uncomfortable, as it *unsettled their historical, cultural, psychological assumptions,* by disrupting the comfortable relationship of words and things, by bringing to a crisis their relation with language and with reality.

Michel Foucault called this linguisic disruption or displacement, **an heterotopia**, and in *Les Mots et les Choses* he put it this way: *Heterotopia disturbs, no doubt because it secretly undermines language, because it prevents this or that to be named, because it destroys or confuses the meaning of* *common words, because it ruins syntax in advance, not only the syntax that constructs sentences, but that less visible syntax that holds words and things together.* [My translation]

As the theoreticians of literature have demonstrated in the past few years, all works of literature can be viewed from two perspectives: constructively or deconstructively. To borrow two useful terms from Roland Barthes, all works of literature can be viewed as **studium** or as **punctum**. The **studium** approach to a work of art determines its cultural, and even its social context. The **studium** is the source of the viewer/reader's usually mild, polite interest in a text, the same sort of vague, casual, irresponsible interest one takes in certain people, objects, clothes, various forms of entertainment which one finds to be simply *all right*. In other words, an interest without excitement. The **punctum** approach breaks through this complacency of response, thus provoking a more intense and personal (subjective) reaction in the reader. Moreover, the **studium** sends the reader back to the predictable reference, back to the referential terms which made the work of fiction possible, but in which the reader, in fact, has little interest. The **punctum**, on the contrary, locks the reader into the text and gives him both a sense of excitement and discovery, but also a sense of discomfort and anxiety. The **studium** gives statisfaction for recognizing what one already knows—it produces the comfort of easy recognition. The **punctum** represents the encounter with the unknown, with the unpredictable—it causes the agony of unrecognition.

However, if one must choose between easy recognition and the agony of unrecognition, the **punctum** approach is preferable, for as Postmodernism has clearly demonstrated, history is a fiction already told and cancelled, a bad dream already dreamt and forgotten, particularly in the Western World which, for centuries, has been seeking a form of agony worthy of its past.

The denial or dismissal of any avant-garde activity is, of course, the usual method of disposing of what discomforts, what unsettles, of what creates a crisis.

No doubt the end of Postmodernism, which of course corresponds to the end of the avant-garde, has changed considerably the conditions of labor in literature. But I am not of those who believe that this situation brings an end to experimentation, or an end to the exigency of the new and the innovative. I am not ready—and I am sure I speak now for many of my fellow Postmodernists or Surfictionists—to renounce the urgency of innovation, and simply abandon literature to neo-realistic forms, predigested by mass media demands. I do not think that literature can submit that easily to **the possible.** On the contrary, I know that literature, today as always, faces **the impossible,** faces the inadequation of language and of thought to apprehend or even comprehend reality, and yet, always in quest of new forms, literature will succeed in giving life once again to the impossible. Where, and when, and by whom? That I am not ready to say, for we are today still in the same confused predicament which forced Samuel Beckett's Unnamable to ask, some fifty years ago on the threshold of his own tale, and the threhold of Postmodernism: *Where Now? Who Now? When Now?*

Still, one should ask: does Postmodernism have any future? And the answer could be both No and Yes, since by its very nature and definition it existed and performed in a kind of futurity, in the POST-(modern), even the POST-(contemporary). In fact, one should no longer speak of Postmodernism, but of Post-futurism. But leaving aside these useless verbal games, perhaps it is time to discard such terms as **Past, Present, Future,** and replace these with **Before, Now, After,** with the understanding that the **NOW** is no longer a fixed point in time (the present, our present), but a moment in constant shift in relation to what happens before and what happens after. In this sense the term Postmodernism may indeed disappear, though the ideas and innovations of Postmodernism may continue to have validity. After all, isn't it the fate of all **ISMS** to be already obsolete the moment they are articulated?

Nazism, Fascism, Communism, but also Futurism, Surrealism, Existentialism, and all the other Isms of recent history were based on a retroactive ideology or aesthetic, and whatever is retroactive can only inspire itself of a violence and a decadence already nostalgic when it happens. All **Isms** are retroactive scenarios of power and of death already played out at the very moment when they appear in history. And that was also the fate of Postmodernism which, in the last resort, was the sign of a simulation of a decaying movement, the sign of what had been, of what had already passed—that is to say Modernism.

That is why Postmodern fiction, even though called an avant-garde movement, was such a mystifying, and yet necessary historic retroversion. But of course, one's critical response to Postmodern fiction depends on whether one approaches it from the **studium** or the **punctum**.

It is true, however, that using terms such as Postmodern and Avant-garde in the same context immediately raises some complex and ambiguous issues, largely because certain events within Postmodern culture have tended to blur the distinction between avant-garde and mainstream art. This interaction of mainstream and avant-garde started during the eighties when the traditional distinction between high-art and pop-art became a central defining feature of Postmodernism itself. Today such distinction is, if anything, even more difficult to maintain.

For instance, should rock videos by Madonna, Peter Gabriel, or Laurie Anderson be considered mainstrain simply because they are enormously popular, even though they employ visual and verbal techniques that twenty-five years ago would have certainly been considered highly experimental, and therefore Postmodern? Is William Gibson's cyber-punk novel *Neuromancer* avant-garde and therefore Postmodern since it uses unusual formal techniques (collage, cut-ups, appropriation of other texts, bizarre new vocabulary and metaphors, temporal displacement, etc.)? Or does its publication and success in the science-fiction domain establish it as a pop novel? Are television shows like *Max Headroom*, some of the early *Saturday Night Live*, or David Lynch's recent *Twin Peaks* series to be categorized as avant-garde underground works because they utilize many features associated with Postmodern innovations, or as Popular Art because they are in fact merely television shows?

These are complex questions. And facing such questions one should definitely abandon the term Postmodern to describe these activities. Or else invent a new term such as POST-POMO or AVANT-POP, as someone has already proposed.

What makes such questions and distinctions increasingly meaningless has to do with the rise of the media culture and the changes in the way art (including literature) is manufactured, bought, and sold. Specifically, as the market economy (Capitalism in other words) has expanded its operations into previously untapped areas, or areas which at one time were considered unmarketable, it recognized (and of course took advantage of this situation) that there is a significant and potentially profitable audience-market for even the most innovative, radical, shocking, disturbing, unsettling works of art, even those works of art whose avowed purpose is the demolition of the capitalist system itself.

Hence the seeming anomaly of The Sex Pistols' dadaesque brand of enraged anarchy, utter nihilism, violence and pure noise being successfully marketed in England and in the United States. But there are many other equally unusual and revealing examples: Derek Pell's darkly humorous and bitingly satiric collage-and-text works, *Dr. Bey's Suicide Handbook, Dr. Bey's Book of Strange Curiosities, Dr. Bey's Book of the Dead*, all published by a major New York publisher, Avon Books; the gradual rise to literary stardom of Kathy Acker, whose nightmarish punk novels (all derived from Postmodern techniques) such as *Blood and Guts in Hight School, Great Expectations, Empire of the Senseless*, and *In Memorium to Identity* are among the angriest and most graphic treatments of sexuality and violence published in the U.S. in this century; but there is also the commercial success enjoyed by movies like *Blue Velvet*, David Lynch's surreal and disturbing portrayal of the violence and sadomasochism that lies, barely concealed, beneath the bland surfaces of America's suburban dreams; the equally unlikely success enjoyed by performance artist Laurie Anderson, whose quirky blend of experimental minimalist music, stand-up comedy, fragmented lyrics of found language, and the use of odd instruments (a violin that plays human voices, a vocoder that electronically alters human voices) became popular concert attractions and best-selling albums.

All of these in many ways can be considered Postmodern works. But even the controversial novel, *American Psycho*, by Bret Eston Ellis, for better or for worse, is a product of Postmodernism. As a decent citizen, reader and writer, were I to condescent to read such a book, I would fully expect to hate it, and to find it totally boring and not worthy of any intelligent reaction. Yet, curiosity drove me to that novel, and I read a good portion of it (I stopped before the end since I was not really interested to find out how such gruesome stories are resolved). Nevertheless, it turns out that Ellis has actually written a rather interesting novel, somewhat experimental in its narrative technique. It is a funny, obsessive novel, full of memorable voices, and of course, extremely vicious, violent, disturbing, unsettling. And yet, it may be the best book, or at least the most revealing book written about the eighties Republican/Wall Street/Me Too/Rich and Famous/ Greed/Cheat/Gulf-War America. No doubt Ellis, like the rest of the Brat-Pack, and most of the Cyberpunk Fiction writers (William Gibson, Bruce Sterling, Marc Laidlaw, Rudy Rucker) or the new young thugs of innovative fiction, Kathy Acker, Mark Leyner, Mark Amerika, William Vollmann, Eurudice, Criss Mazza, and several others newly arrived on the literary scene, grew up during the Postmodern era and learned their tricks from the old masters and makers of Postmodernism: William Burroughs, Kurt Vonnegut Jr., Thomas Pynchon, Joseph McElroy, John Barth, Donald Barthelme, and many others.

But then, that Post-Pomo generation—these **bright and risen angels**, to play on the title of a recent and fascinating novel by one of these Post-Pomo writers, William T. Vollmann—has as much right to its vision of reality, however twisted or preposterous or virtual it may be, as the previous generation.

This anomaly of the popularity of an art which openly and defiantly denounces what makes it live, of an art that bites the hand that feeds it, is not only evident in literature, but in much of the visual arts too, and of course in the new Rock Music, in Rap, in MTV, which consists of non-sequential, rapid fire profusion of disjointed bits of images and informations thrown in the face of the capitalistic system.

But why shouldn't these new writers and artists not live in their time and be shaped by their time: the era of computer, fax, video, telecommunication—but also the era of greed and fraudulence.

The Postmodernists of the 1960s and 1970s reached the age of reason (or unreason) in the 1940s and 1950s, and their intellectual and aesthetic sensibilities were shaped by Existentialism and Structuralism, by the Beats, Jazz (especially Bebop), Abstract Expressionim, and the appearance, at least in the United States of authors such as Kafka, Nabokov, Borges, Beckett. Today, the cultural matrix that produced the first wave of Postmodern fiction seems as distant and old-fashioned to us as love-beads, incense, communes, flower-people, and phrases like: *turn on, tune in, drop out.*

Though no one ever really felt comfortable with the term Postmodern, nonetheless for several decades it served to define a certain avant-garde activity played out on a high intellectual and artistic level, at times even accused of being elitist, until that activity was absorbed into mainstream culture by the economy and quickly turned into Pop-Art. And so now it is time, perhaps, to abandon the term Postmodern.

Octavio Paz may have, in fact, put an end to all further discussions of Postmodernism when in his acceptance speech for the 1990 Nobel Prize he reflected on the elusive meaning of the concept of modernity.

What is modernity? It is, first of all, an ambiguous term: there are as many types of modernity as there are societies. Each society has its own. The meaning of the word is as uncertain and arbitrary as the name of the period that precedes it, the Middle-Ages. If we are modern when compared to medieval times, are we perhaps the Middle-Ages of a future Modernity? Is a name that changes with time a real name? Modernity is a word in search of its meaning. Is it an idea, a mirage or a moment of history? Nobody knows for sure . . . In recent years there has been much talk of Postmodernism, but what is Postmodernism if not an even more modern modernity? [my emphasis]

Octavio Paz may be right. Postmodernism has now become the Middle-Ages of the next, as yet unnamed, era. But while waiting for that era to be named, discussed, debated, argued, explained, dismissed, so that it may in turn become the Middle-Ages of the subsequent era, let us admit that Postmodernism was a great fun adventure. It is only too bad that all the explorers involved in that adventure could not have survived to see **The End**.

I began this essay by quoting from Beckett's *Stirrings Still*, I would like to close with another few words from that last gasp of Postmodern fiction—a passage which seems to describe so well the present predicament of the Postmodern writer:

Head on hands half hoping when he disappeared again that he would not reappear again and half fearing that he would not. Or merely wondering. Or merely waiting. Waiting to see if he would or would not.

What puzzles me about this presentation (part 1 as well as part 2) is that in attempting to explain how **Postmodernism** came to an end, I may have, in fact, written yet another postmodern text. Oh well! As Beckett's Unnamable once put:

Here all is clear . . . No all is not clear . . . but the discourse must go on . . . so one invents obscurities . . . RHETORIC.

Breinigsville, PA USA
09 December 2009
228959BV00001B/116/A